Mastering the Art of Chinese Cooking

Charmaine Solomon

McGraw-Hill Book Company

New York St. Louis
San Francisco Toronto

The Publishers would like to thank the following for
their kind assistance in lending us props for photography:
Doulton Tableware Pty Ltd, Gordon N.S.W.
Mikasa Tableware Pty Ltd, Glebe N.S.W.
Kosta Boda Australia Pty Ltd, Artarmon N.S.W.
Tee Jay Antiques, Willoughby N.S.W.
We'd particularly like to thank William Lai of
Asia Provisions Pty Ltd, Chatswood N.S.W.
for all his help in the preparation of this book.

Food styled by June Budgen

Photographer Ray Joyce

1 2 3 4 5 6 7 8 9   8 7 6 5 4

ISBN 0-07-059655-7

First published in Australia in 1984 by Lansdowne, Sydney a division of
RPLA Pty Limited
176 South Creek Road, Dee Why West, N.S.W., Australia, 2099.
First U.S. publication in 1984 by the McGraw-Hill Book Company.
Copyright © 1984 by Charmaine Solomon.

Library of Congress Cataloging-in-Publication Data

Solomon, Charmaine.
Mastering the art of Chinese cooking.
1. Cookery, Chinese. I. Title.
TX 724.5.C5S63 1984   641.5951   84-12229

Contents

Introduction

Chinese cooking has long been acknowledged as the most sophisticated of all the great cuisines. It is also the most ingenious.

The amazing variety of ingredients were first used in sheer necessity. The country has always been subject to drought and flood and only a small proportion of the land is suitable for agriculture, so the people have learned to make use of everything edible. Who else but the Chinese have made a delicacy from wood fungus, birds' nests and fish's maw?

Chinese food should appeal to all the senses. First there is visual impact. Colour and form are considered in the combination of ingredients and the shapes they are cut into. On special occasions, the Chinese delight in garnishes made from vegetables and representing flowers, butterflies, birds or animals. The fragrance of a dish is important, for before the food can give pleasure by its taste, it should whet the appetite with its aroma.

Some dishes are prized for the noise they make – such as sizzling rice – but it has other attractions – the crispness of the rice itself and the flavour of the sauce served with it.

A dissertation on texture ingredients in a classic essay on Chinese gastronomy differentiates between crunchy, smooth, elastic, chewy, soft, resilient, spongy, melting, grainy, unctuous, fibrous, gelatinous. Many of these qualities would be lost on even the most discerning western gourmet. Some of the most highly regarded foods are totally devoid of flavour but are prized because of their texture. Skilful cooking imbues them with appeal from the seasonings they are combined with.

Finally, and most important of all, is the taste of the food. There are many effects to strive for. Some dishes are supposed to be light, delicate and natural in flavour but without being insipid. Others are prized for their rich, concentrated flavour.

Choosing a menu

A Chinese meal does not feature one main dish, but rather a number of dishes of equal importance. A cleverly chosen menu presents contrasting dishes, so the qualities of each are set off by the others.

A formal banquet is served as a succession of courses with pauses in between for drinking, conversation and playing games – which explains how diners can partake of ten or more courses and how banquets can last for hours. Indeed, in times gone by, they lasted for days!

When planning a Chinese menu, be guided by the rules that apply to Western meals – don't repeat main ingredients or flavours, balance a rich dish with a light one, serve vegetables on their own if they are not featured with the meat or seafood. Remember that steamed rice is important because most Chinese dishes taste better with it.

Until you become really proficient in the split-second timing required for stir-frying, don't be tempted to present more than one dish cooked by this method. Include roasted, boiled and braised dishes that may be cooked ahead and reheated – not only because it's easier on the chef, but for more variety.

At family meals or for informal entertaining, all the dishes are placed on the table at once. This makes it unnecessary for the hostess to leave the table once the meal has started. Each person has a bit of each dish with rice. Soup is not served at the start of a meal, as in western-style eating, but in banquets is served between other courses. In family-style meals it is placed on the table and everyone helps themselves, just as they do with rice. It is not necessary to have one dish for each diner.

Above: *a Chinese place setting: bowl and porcelain spoon, bone plate, chopsticks on chopstick rest, sauce dishes.*

Right: *typical Chinese teapot and teacups. In background, cane basket for carrying teapot and keeping it warm.*

Right: *chopsticks with rests.*

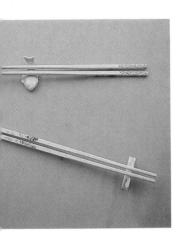

Chinese place settings

Chinese food may be served in any dish of appropriate size, but for eating try to provide each person with a small bowl, and chopsticks and a porcelain spoon. It is easier to pick up food from a bowl than from a flat plate, and the 10 cm (4 inch) size does for both solid food and soups.

The bowl is placed on a small flat plate, which is the 'bone plate' – a place where the small bones may conveniently be discarded.

Small individual-size sauce dishes are useful and in some dishes quite essential, as the food is given flavour with the dipping sauce.

Porcelain spoons are favoured not merely because they can be bought in colours to match the bowls, but for the very practical reason that they do not get hot as metal spoons do and diners run less risk of burning their lips when supping the very hot soups. Chopstick rests are a nice touch, although not absolutely essential.

The Chinese teacup is small, without handles, and looks right for serving and drinking Chinese tea at the end of a meal. Hefty western-style cups with handles somehow don't seem appropriate.

If serving Chinese wine with the meal, it is usually served warm. Small flasks in which it can be warmed (by standing the flask in hot water) come with half a dozen wine cups in the set.

Cooking methods

Chinese cooking may, at first glance, appear difficult and far removed from everyday methods in a western-style kitchen.

But there are many cooking methods which are familiar to the western cook – boiling, braising, stewing, simmering, steaming, deep frying. Not as well known is cooking in stored heat, which takes longer but makes good sense because it saves fuel and yields good results.

Then there is the quick stir-frying method which always fascinates the newcomer to Chinese cooking. It looks very impressive but there is nothing to it except split-second timing and this is easily mastered with a little practice. All that is necessary is to have every ingredient prepared and ready within reach before starting to cook, because there is no time to go looking for a sauce or seasoning once cooking is under way.

It is for this method of cooking, in particular, that food is cut into paper-thin slices or slivers because the cooking time is so short. The principle is that the ingredients which require longer cooking go into the wok first, to be followed in turn by the others. It originated out of the need to save fuel, and that is as good a reason to use this method today as it was centuries ago.

Then there are recipes in which more than one method is used. This is called cross-cooking or combination cooking. A duck may be steamed until tender, then boned and cut into pieces and deep fried so that the outside is crisp and crackling, the inner portions meltingly soft. Or bite-size pieces of poultry, meat or seafood may be briefly deep fried and set aside, and just before serving they are stir-fried with other ingredients and seasonings.

Roasting is not a common cooking method in China, where homes do not have ovens and the method is too wasteful of fuel, but because oven cooking is so convenient in western kitchens, some restaurant recipes have been adapted for this book.

Utensils and preparation methods

With a sharp Chinese chopper, a heavy cleaver and a stout wooden chopping block, anyone can master the art of slicing, chopping and cutting in the Chinese way. Cleavers and choppers may look clumsy but they are surprisingly com-

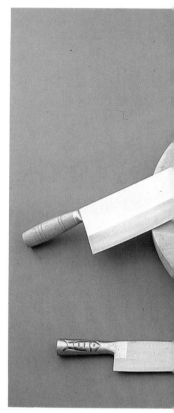

fortable to handle and, as long as they are kept in good condition, are safe to use. A sharp knife is safer than a blunt one, providing it is used with an awareness of its sharp edge.

Chopping through bones is often called for in preparing poultry or meat. With a heavy cleaver held firmly where the handle joins the blade, and an unhesitating delivery, this task can be accomplished without difficulty. Since in this book we have the advantage of every recipe illustrated in photographs, there is no need to try to explain about diagonal cutting, shredding and other methods. Each one can be clearly seen.

A sturdy wooden chopping block or board is a must. Please do not use slick-surfaced lightweight chopping boards, no matter how decorative they are. Hang them on your kitchen wall if you must, but chop on solid wood. It will save your knife blades and save many a dangerous situation too, because its surface is not smooth and slippery. To be safe and effective the chopping block must be at least 5 cm (2 inches) thick and large enough to allow room to work freely.

There are different kinds of choppers. Stainless steel looks good but carbon steel holds a better edge and is easier to sharpen. A good compromise is the type in which the blade is of stainless steel enclosing a cutting edge of carbon steel. Like the wok, choppers must be washed and thoroughly dried before putting away, especially if made of carbon steel.

The most useful chopper is that with a large rectangular blade. The handle of the chopper is useful for pounding or crushing, taking the place of a pestle. The side of the blade is used for crushing garlic or flattening a circle of pastry to a thin, translucent sheet. The pointed corner takes over from the tip of the chef's knife. And the large rectangular blade is just the thing to carry cut ingredients from chopping block to wok.

Above: *wooden chopping boards and choppers.*

What to cook on

Quick, high, instantly controllable heat is what makes Chinese cooking a pleasure, so gas is therefore the most suitable fuel. But there are ways of using electricity to advantage. One is to buy a flat-bottomed wok – an invention which takes into account the fact that people in Asian countries who live in modern blocks of flats have to cook with electricity. The flat base gives better contact with the hotplate and prevents wobbling. The high, flaring sides of the wok enable the cook to toss, flip and stir without ingredients being scattered as may happen in a conventional frying pan or skillet.

Electricity is not flexible like gas, and different methods have to be used to achieve the same results. With an electric stove, heat one hotplate on the highest setting, put the wok on it and let it get very hot before adding the oil and ingredients to be cooked. When less heat is needed, lift the wok off the hotplate (turning the heat down would not reduce it quickly enough). If the dish needs simmering after the initial cooking on high heat, have another hotplate ready on simmer setting and transfer the wok to this.

If you can get only round-bottomed woks, use a metal collar or ring which will hold the wok in place and steady it. These rings are sometimes necessary even on gas stoves, depending on the design. It is essential you should feel confident that the wok is held steady.

The rings are usually made of anodized aluminium and are constructed with sloping sides so one opening is smaller than the other. There are holes in the ring to allow ventilation. When high heat is required, use the ring with the large opening upwards so that the wok sits close to the source of heat. When simmering, the smaller opening should be uppermost so that the wok is held higher up and further away from the heat.

If cooking for a number of people, remember to cook two batches of the dish rather than double the quantities. This applies to stir-fried dishes especially, for if too much is added to the wok at a time, the heat will not be sufficient to seal the juices in and the food will stew rather than fry.

What to cook in

There is no doubt that cooking Chinese food in a wok is as appropriate as eating Chinese food with chopsticks. While it is possible to cook Chinese food in other types of pans, the wok was designed specifically for Chinese cooking and really does make it easier. Especially when stir-frying, the high, flaring sides enable food to be stirred and tossed with speed and allows meat to be pressed against the hot metal to seal the surfaces. The food unmistakably tastes better.

Any Chinese cook will confirm that a well-used wok develops what is known as 'wok hay' – a sort of character of its own, which adds an extra dimension to food cooked in it, just as the well-aged clay pots used in some other countries give a special flavour to food.

Woks come in many sizes. I would recommend one 35 cm (14 inches) in diameter as being suitable for domestic use. It may look large and can cook enough for 6 to 8 people. Even if you don't usually cook for that many, consider that whereas you can cook small amounts in a large wok, you can't cook large amounts in a small wok.

Some woks have a long wooden handle, but the original design has two rounded handles and I find this easier to use when lifting the wok as the weight is more evenly distributed.

Below: *wok and bamboo brush for cleaning wok.*

A word about those handles. They do get quite hot in the course of cooking. Chinese chefs use a cloth, folded many times to form a heatproof pad. It becomes second nature to them to reach for the wok with pads in hand, but for the amateur home cook it takes a bit of practice to remember. I take precautions by wrapping the metal handles in two or three layers of insulating tape. This way, even if I grab the handles, no blistered fingers result. After a couple of months of constant use, the tape does become tacky and must be replaced but it is a small chore well worth performing.

When buying a wok, don't imagine that the most expensive is the best. Forget the stainless steel or aluminium woks, the non-stick linings, all the gimmickry that crops up whenever something becomes popular. These are woks in name only. Look for the original iron woks, or the serviceable enamelled wok in our photographs. A 35 cm (14 in) wok should weigh about 1 kilogram. Those intended for use on electric hotplates are heavier in order to make good contact and have a small flat area in the base.

When new, a wok must be cleaned and seasoned. Most iron woks have a coating to prevent them rusting during transportation and storage. This is a stubborn film which must be removed by filling the wok with hot water and adding 2 tablespoons of bicarbonate of soda (baking soda); bring to the boil and simmer for 20 minutes. This softens the coating which can then be scrubbed off with a fine scourer. Repeat the process if necessary. This is the first and last time you should scour the wok.

Seasoning the wok

Having cleaned the wok thoroughly, season it. This is very important because it creates a smooth surface which prevents food from sticking, becoming discoloured, or absorbing a metallic taste from the 'raw' metal.

Heat the wok and wipe over the entire inner surface with a wad of kitchen paper dipped in peanut oil. At first, the paper will turn rusty and brown. Repeat with more paper and more oil. After a number of times the paper will not become brown. Allow the wok to cool, rinse it with warm water, then repeat the heating and rubbing with oil as before.

The wok is now ready to cook in. Remember the rule, 'hot wok, warm oil'. Make sure the wok is thoroughly heated before adding the oil, and wait for the oil to become hot before adding ingredients. Then food will not stick to the wok but will slide easily over the surface.

After use, wash the wok in hot water and scrub it gently with a dish mop or sponge. Do not scour with steel wool or scouring powder. If necessary, fill it with hot water and leave it to soak and soften any food that may have cooked on, then scrub with a brush.

The wok should always be completely dry before it is put away. To ensure this, place it over the source of heat until any moisture has completely vaporized. **Wiping with a dish cloth is simply not enough.**

If not used often, the wok should be wiped over lightly with a piece of kitchen paper dipped in peanut oil to prevent rust, but only after it has been dried over heat. Don't store the wok in a closed cupboard – it would develop a musty odour. Hang it near the stove, both to keep it in usable condition and to remind you how versatile a utensil it is, for frequent use.

Above: *nest of bamboo steaming baskets.*

Wok accessories and other utensils

When you buy a wok, buy a lid for it too. It is necessary when braising, simmering or steaming, and should fit snugly inside the wok. Choose a high dome-shaped lid as this will accommodate larger items such as a whole duck or chicken. These lids are generally made from lightweight aluminium and dent easily, so treat with care.

Other accessories are a steaming rack or steaming baskets. The former is a simple arrangement of bamboo, wood or metal which holds food above water level. A wire cake rack (round, of course) is a good substitute.

Steaming can be done in a large saucepan if you have one with a well-fitting lid. The plate of food is placed on a trivet or an upturned heatproof bowl to hold it above water level. The plate should be of a size that allows steam to circulate.

For steaming more than one kind of food at a time, it is best to use an aluminium steamer with multiple layers, or a nest of bamboo steamers. The bamboo steamers are particularly useful if you want to cook dim sum – dumplings, buns and patties. The woven bamboo lid with its natural perforations prevents condensation forming on the inner surface, falling on to the buns and spoiling their appearance. This can happen with metal steamers, but placing a clean dry tea towel across the top before covering with the lid solves the problem of condensation.

A sandy pot, or earthenware casserole, is ideal for slow-simmered dishes and is quite picturesque for presenting food in. The outside is a creamy colour and the inside is glazed dark brown. It comes in varying sizes and with one or two handles. It should not be placed over heat without first putting some liquid in it. When ingredients have to be browned first, this is done in a wok and they are then transferred to the pot for simmering.

The Yunnan pot is another beautifully shaped cooking vessel which has an unusual feature – a small funnel in the centre which allows steam into the pot. I love its rounded shape and the way it cooks the most delicately flavoured soup.

Then there is the steamboat (hotpot) which cooks at the table from live coals piled into its central funnel. Small wire cooking spoons are used to suspend pieces of food in the simmering stock, or wooden chopsticks may be substituted to hold the food as it cooks. An electric deep fryer or electric wok or a

tabletop cooker with a vessel on it may be used instead, but for atmosphere and authenticity there's nothing to beat the steamboat itself, even if it is more trouble filling the chimney with live coals than simply plugging in and flicking a switch. Remember to have the coals prepared an hour or more beforehand so that they are well aglow before transferring them to the steamboat; and have the moat filled with stock before doing so.

Cooking implements

There is a frying spoon called a wok chan which is shaped to fit into the curve of the wok. It is exactly right for the tossing, flipping and pressing motions that take place during stir-frying. Stainless steel is the most suitable metal. When transferring food from the wok, the slight curve on its leading edge and the upturned edges on the other two sides make it very practical. A curved frying spoon may be substituted, but because of the slots it is not as useful in transferring cooked food and sauces.

A ladle is handy because it doubles as a measure. Choose one which holds a half cup of liquid. Once the eye is trained to levels in its bowl, it can be used to speedily dip out stock or water in the amounts required.

For deep frying, a large twisted-wire draining spoon with flat wooden handle is extremely useful. Buy one large enough to hold a whole fish. It is handy for smaller items as well. When frying small pieces of food, it is easy to skim them out on this strainer.

There is another shape of twisted-wire spoon – a deep cup shape, which is used for holding food such as noodles or dumplings in bubbling broth until heated and lifting all the food out at once, as in wonton soup.

Below: *from left: sandy pot, woks with draining rack and lid, wire frying spoons and cup-shaped wire ladle for dipping noodles, metal ladle, wok chan, wooden rice spoon.*

Appetizers and Savoury Snacks

Most formal banquets start with appetizers. A trend that has also become popular, even when having just a simple meal in a Chinese restaurant, is to assuage the pangs of hunger until the main dishes arrive by ordering a plate or two of hot dim sum. These are usually enclosed in fine pastry and either steamed or fried.

Originating with the chefs of the Sung Dynasty, these little mouthfuls were intended as delicacies and culinary showpieces to impress guests. Dim sum literally means 'touch the heart'. Gradually they were aspired to by the merchant class and eventually by the working class. Now they are so popular with all manner of people that in Chinese cities (or Chinese quarters of western cities) whole families, from grandparents to babes in arms, gather at restaurants on a Sunday morning especially, for yum cha (tea) or dim sum brunch.

The concept of a dim sum meal grew up around the Chinese tea house where people met to talk, read newspapers, or simply refuel. I have been at dim sum restaurants as early as seven in the morning and have been told that the trade starts at about 4 a.m. as Chinese workers from night shifts come in for cup after cup of hot tea and an endless variety of small savoury dishes. By eight in the morning, these places close. It is then that the more elegant restaurants start serving their dim sum to the leisured classes who rise later. At working-class tea houses the dim sum are actually quite hearty, not dainty as at fashionable restaurants.

Waitresses circulate among the crowded tables with trolleys or trays bearing steaming baskets, plates and bowls. In them or on them is an incredible variety of dim sum. Customers look them over and choose whatever appeals, and at the end of the meal the waitress counts the empty dishes and calculates the bill.

The recipes in this chapter are for some of the most popular appetizers and snacks. Shaping the pastries may require a little practice, but that applies to most pastries, Chinese or otherwise.

Left: *clockwise from left: Steamed dumplings; Chinese mushrooms; sheets of green bean starch; water chestnuts; red vinegar for dipping; Prawn dumplings in Transparent Pastry (see page 16); chilli sauce for dipping; sesame seeds; Steamed Pearl Balls (see page 29); bottles of oyster sauce and sesame oil; rock sugar; Spring Rolls (see page 24).*

Deep Fried Chicken and Ham Rolls

Remove skin from the chicken breasts, and with a sharp knife, bone the breasts. Divide each whole breast in two down the middle. On the underside of the flesh, next to the bone, there is a small cylindrical fillet which lifts off easily; reserve this for another dish. Put the large pieces of breast between two sheets of freezer plastic and pound until thin, using the smooth side of a meat mallet and taking care not to tear the flesh.

Combine salt, five spice powder and garlic; spread this evenly on the inside of each piece of breast.

Cut the ham into sticks 12 mm (½ inch) wide and the length of the chicken breast. Shave the corners to round the sticks. Place a stick of ham on each piece of breast and roll up to enclose the ham completely, moulding the chicken flesh to seal.

Dip in the beaten egg, then into the flour. Put diagonally on a spring roll wrapper, roll over twice, then fold in the corners, envelope fashion. Seal the pastry with a little beaten egg mixed to a thick paste with flour.

Heat 4 cups of oil in a wok and fry two rolls at a time for about 3 or 4 minutes, turning the rolls with tongs so that they brown evenly. Drain on absorbent paper.

Cut into diagonal slices and arrange on a bed of shredded lettuce. Serve with Sweet and Sour Sauce for dipping, if liked.

Sweet and Sour Sauce: The red food colouring powder is available from Chinese food stores, and only the smallest amount is required. Place the sugar and vinegar in a small saucepan. Add ¾ cup (6 fl oz) water and bring to the boil. Use a skewer to put a small quantity of the food colouring into the sauce. Blend cornflour with 1 tablespoon of cold water and stir this into the sauce until it boils and thickens. Add salt and mix in well.

Serves 6–8
2 large breasts of chicken
¼ teaspoon salt
¼ teaspoon five spice powder
¼ teaspoon crushed garlic
1 slice ham 12 mm (½ inch) thick
2 eggs, beaten
flour for coating
4 large sheets spring roll pastry
oil for deep frying
shredded lettuce for serving
Sweet and Sour Sauce:
½ cup (4 oz) sugar
½ cup (4 fl oz) white vinegar
red food colouring powder
1 tablespoon cornflour (cornstarch)
¼ teaspoon salt

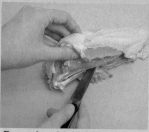
Bone the chicken breasts.

Place ham stick on flattened chicken breast.

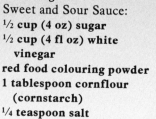

Fold corners of wrapper over chicken roll.

Prawn Toast

Serves 6

6 square slices white bread
250 g (8 oz) raw prawns
1 egg, beaten
**½ teaspoon finely grated
   fresh ginger**
½ teaspoon salt
1 tablespoon oyster sauce
**2 teaspoons cornflour
   (cornstarch)**
**sprigs of fresh coriander
   (Chinese parsley)**
**2 tablespooons sesame
   seeds**
peanut oil for deep frying

Serve as a tasty appetizer with drinks, as part of a meal, between courses, or as a snack.

TRIM THE CRUSTS off the bread, cut each slice in half diagonally or into three strips, and leave on a tray for an hour or two to dry out a little.

Shell and de-vein the prawns. If using frozen prawns, thaw completely and drain off any liquid. Chop the prawns very finely and place in a bowl. Add 1 tablespoon of the beaten egg, the ginger, salt, oyster sauce and cornflour; mix well to blend to a smooth paste.

Spread the bread with prawn mixture. Press a sprig of coriander on some of the pieces. Brush other pieces lightly with the remaining beaten egg, and dip in sesame seeds to coat.

Heat the oil for deep frying and when hot, put in a few pieces of bread at a time, prawn side downwards. Fry until the bread is golden, lift out on wire spoon and allow to drain on absorbent paper. Serve hot.

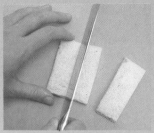

Cut bread into strips.

Spread bread with prawn mixture.

Dip some of the bread into sesame seeds.

Prawn Dumplings in Transparent Pastry

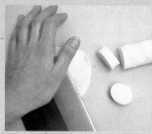

Flatten slice of dough with Chinese chopper.

Flute and join edges of dough.

Steam dumplings on oiled greaseproof paper in Chinese basket.

Filling: Shell and de-vein the prawns and cut into small pieces. Combine with all the other ingredients for the filling, mixing thoroughly. Set aside while making the dough.

Dough: Mix the Chinese wheat flour and cornflour together in a bowl. Put the measured water and the lard into a small saucepan and bring to the boil. Remove from heat and cool while counting 20 seconds, then pour all at once on to the flour. Mix well with chopsticks or the handle of a wooden spoon, and as soon as it is cool enough to handle, knead to a smooth, pliable dough.

Divide into two equal portions and mould each into a cylinder 2.5 cm (1 inch) in diameter. Wrap the dough in plastic film to prevent the surface drying out.

Cut one of the cylinders of dough into 10 equal slices and re-cover these with plastic wrap. On a smooth surface (a laminated pastry board is ideal), flatten one dough slice with the lightly greased blade of a wide Chinese chopper to a round about 10 cm (4 inches) in diameter.

Put a teaspoonful of filling on the dough. Bring the edges of the dough together over the filling, pinch to seal, and at the same time flute the joined edges on one side so that the dumpling has the shape of a bonnet. (Don't worry if the shape is not perfect, it will still taste marvellous!) Repeat with remaining dough and filling.

Brush the dumplings lightly with sesame oil and place each one on an oiled square of greaseproof paper. Steam for 12 minutes. Serve warm, with sauces for dipping.

Makes 20

Filling:
- 250 g (8 oz) raw prawns
- 2 tablespoons finely chopped ham fat
- 2 tablespoons finely chopped bamboo shoot
- 2 spring onions (scallions), finely chopped
- 1/2 teaspoon finely grated fresh ginger
- 3 teaspoons cornflour (cornstarch)
- 1 teaspoon sesame oil
- 1 teaspoon salt
- 1 teaspoon sugar

Dough:
- 1 cup (4 oz) Chinese wheat flour
- 3 tablespoons cornflour (cornstarch)
- 210 ml (7 fl oz) water
- 1 tablespoon lard
- sesame oil for brushing

Butterfly Prawns

Slit prawns along back, flatten gently.

Coat with cornflour, egg and breadcrumbs.

Shell and devein the prawns, leaving the tails intact.

With a sharp knife, slit the prawns along curve of the back but do not cut right through. Flatten gently. Combine soy sauce, wine, garlic crushed with salt, ginger. Marinate the prawns in this mixture for 15 minutes.

Dip the prawns into cornflour, shake off excess, then dip into the beaten egg and finally into the breadcrumbs. Press gently to flatten the prawns again and to firm on the crumb coating. Chill for 30 minutes.

Heat a wok, add oil and when hot, fry the prawns, two or three at a time, until golden brown (about 2 minutes). Drain on kitchen paper and serve hot, with chilli sauce if desired. Garnish with lemon butterflies.

Serves 4–6
12 large raw prawns
2 tablespoons light soy
   sauce
1 tablespoon Chinese wine
   or dry sherry
1 small clove garlic,
   crushed
¼ teaspoon salt
½ teaspoon finely grated
   fresh ginger
½ cup cornflour
   (cornstarch)
1 large egg, beaten
breadcrumbs for coating
peanut oil for deep frying
lemon 'butterflies' for
   garnishing

Steamed Dumplings

Makes about 24

**6 dried Chinese
mushrooms**
**500 g (1 lb) small raw
prawns**
6 canned water chestnuts
3 spring onions (scallions)
**3 tablespoons chopped
bamboo shoot**
**250 g (8 oz) minced
(ground) pork**
1½ teaspoons salt
**1 tablespoon light soy
sauce**
**1 tablespoon Chinese wine
or dry sherry**
1 teaspoon sesame oil
1 egg white
**125 g (4 oz) wonton
wrappers**

Place the mushrooms in hot water; soak for 30 minutes.

Peel the prawns, reserve about 24 for garnish, and chop the remainder. Drain the mushrooms; slice off and discard their stems. Chop the mushroom caps, water chestnuts and spring onions. Combine the chopped ingredients with bamboo shoot, pork, salt, soy sauce, wine, sesame oil and egg white; mix well together.

Put 1 heaped teaspoon of the mixture in the centre of each wonton wrapper. Gather the wrapper around the filling and press it together to give the shape of a little money bag, open at the top. Press a reserved prawn on top of each for decoration.

Lightly oil a steamer and place the dumplings in a single layer on the perforated tray. Cover tightly and steam for 20 minutes over boiling water. Serve hot or cold, with a dipping sauce of soy or chilli.

*Chop the mushrooms, water
chestnuts and spring onions.*

*Place mixture on wonton
wrapper.*

*Form dumpling into money
bag shape.*

Chicken and Ham wrapped in Lettuce

Serves 6–8

3 dried mushrooms
500 g (1 lb) chicken thighs
1 chicken liver
125 g (4 oz) ham
1 egg
1 teaspoon cornflour
  (cornstarch)
1 tablespoon light soy
  sauce
4 tablespoons finely
  chopped bamboo shoot
2 spring onions
  (scallions), finely
  chopped
1 teaspoon finely grated
  fresh ginger
2 tablespoons sweet bean
  paste (tim mein jeung)
½ teaspoon salt
1 head lettuce
1 tablespoon peanut oil

Soak the mushrooms in hot water for 30 minutes. Then discard the stems and finely chop the caps.

Remove skin and bones from the chicken. Halve the liver and remove any tubes and discoloured spots. Finely chop the chicken, liver and ham in a food processor or with a chopper. Beat the egg and in a bowl combine the minced mixture, beaten egg, cornflour and soy sauce. Cover the bowl and set aside.

In a separate bowl, combine the chopped mushrooms, bamboo shoot, spring onions and the ginger.

In a third (small) bowl, stir 2 tablespoons of water into the sweet bean paste and add the salt.

Wash the lettuce leaves, trim to a neat shape, wrap in a clean towel, and chill.

Heat a wok, add oil and when hot, stir-fry the chicken mixture for about 3 minutes or until its colour changes. Add vegetables and stir-fry a further 2 minutes. Add the bean paste mixture and stir well together.

Serve the hot filling in a large bowl and the chilled lettuce leaves on a platter or large bowl. Place a spoonful of the mixture on a lettuce leaf, roll up and eat. It is quite in order to use the fingers for this dish.

Note: If liked, fry 3–4 tablespoons of pine nuts in oil until golden, then toss them in with the filling after it has been cooked.

Finely chop the mushrooms, bamboo shoots, spring onions and ginger.

Mix the bean paste with water.

Vegetarian Dumplings

Finely chop the prepared gluten.

Add the cabbage to the wok with the other vegetables.

Press points of dumpling with the back of a teaspoon.

Makes about 24

2 cups cooked and minced gluten (see page 53)
4 dried Chinese mushrooms
2 tablespoons peanut oil
4 spring onions (scallions), finely chopped
1 teaspoon crushed garlic
1 teaspoon finely grated ginger
2 cups finely chopped Chinese cabbage (wongah bak)
10 water chestnuts, chopped
2 tablespoons light soy sauce
2 teaspoons sesame oil
1 teaspoon salt (or to taste)
1 large egg, beaten
1 tablespoon cornflour (cornstarch)
125 g (4 oz) wonton wrappers

Prepare the gluten and when cool, squeeze out excess water and mince in food processor or chop finely.

Soak the mushrooms in hot water for 30 minutes. Then discard the mushroom stems and finely chop the caps.

Heat a wok, add the peanut oil and when the oil is hot, fry the spring onions, garlic and ginger, stirring, for a few seconds until fragrant. Add the cabbage and toss until cabbage is soft. Add water chestnuts, mushrooms and gluten and toss for a minute or two, then transfer the mixture to a large bowl.

Mix together the soy sauce, sesame oil, salt, beaten egg and cornflour. Pour over the gluten mixture and mix well with your hand to distribute the seasonings and bind together.

Place a tablespoon of the mixture in the centre of each wonton wrapper, gather the wrapper to enclose the filling and squeeze the dumpling firmly to make the dough adhere to the filling. Press the points down with the back of a teaspoon.

Place the dumplings in an oiled steamer and steam for 10 minutes. Serve warm, or refrigerate until needed and reheat by steaming for a couple of minutes.

Golden Cuttlefish Balls

Serves 6

2 cups (3 oz) very tiny bread cubes

500 g (1 lb) cleaned cuttlefish (or squid)

1 teaspoon salt

1 teaspoon sugar

1 teaspoon sesame oil

4 cups (1 litre) oil for deep frying

Dipping Sauce:

½ cup (4 fl oz) white vinegar

½ cup (4 fl oz) water or pineapple juice

2 tablespoons sugar

1 tablespoon tomato purée

½ teaspoon salt

1 teaspoon cornflour (cornstarch)

Remove the cuttle-bone.

Roll the cuttlefish balls in the bread cubes.

To prepare the bread cubes, trim the crusts off several thin slices of day-old bread and cut into thin strips, then into tiny dice no more than 4 mm (1/8 inch) each way.

Wash the cuttlefish well and remove any of the fine membrane that may be clinging to the flesh. Chop the cuttlefish finely or mince in food processor using steel chopping blade. Transfer to a bowl and mix in the salt, sugar and sesame oil. Take teaspoons of the mixture and roll into small balls about 2 cm (¾ inch) in diameter.

Spread the bread cubes on a sheet of paper and roll the cuttlefish balls in them until they are covered.

Heat the oil and deep fry the balls, a few at a time, until golden; do not overcook. Drain on absorbent paper and serve warm, with sauce for dipping if liked.

Dipping Sauce: Heat vinegar, water (or pineapple juice), sugar, tomato purée and salt in a small saucepan. When boiling, stir in the cornflour mixed smoothly with 1 tablespoon of cold water. Cook, stirring, until it boils and becomes thick and clear.

Note: Squid may be substituted for cuttlefish. And if a hot sauce is preferred, serve a dip of bottled chilli sauce.

Pot Stickers

Place the mushrooms in hot water; soak for 30 minutes.

Discard the mushroom stems, and chop the caps finely. Finely chop the spring onions, add to the pork, and mix in the mushrooms, bamboo shoot, ginger, salt, soy sauce and sesame oil. Blend the cornflour with 2 tablespoons of cold water and add it to pork mixture, mixing all well together.

Dough: Measure the flour into a large bowl. Pour in the boiling water, stirring with chopsticks (or the handle of a wooden spoon) for a few minutes. As soon as it is cool enough, knead the dough well until it is soft and smooth, dusting with flour if necessary.

Shape the dough into a log, then roll it on a smooth surface into a sausage shape 2.5 cm (1 inch) in diameter. Slice it evenly into 30 pieces. Cover with a damp cloth to prevent it drying.

On a lightly floured board, roll each piece of dough to a circle 8 cm (3¼ inches) in diameter. Make overlapping pleats around one side of the circle. Place a teaspoon of the filling in the centre. Dampen the edges of the dough with water, and pinch them together to seal. Keep the dumplings under a damp cloth but not touching each other as they would stick.

Heat a large heavy flat-bottomed frying pan over a medium heat. Add 2 tablespoons of the peanut oil and when hot, tilt the pan to coat its entire base and a little way up the side. Add half the dumplings, pleated side up. (It is easier to cook them in two batches.) Lift the dumplings with a flat spatula to prevent them sticking, and cook until they are golden underneath.

In a saucepan bring to the boil 1 cup of water and 2 tablespoons of the oil, and pour this over the dumplings. Loosen any that are sticking. Bring the liquid to the boil again, cover the frying pan and cook for 5 minutes; then reduce the heat and cook for a further 5 minutes. Remove the frying pan lid, and cook until liquid evaporates and the dumplings are browned and crusty underneath. Lift the dumplings to prevent sticking.

Cook the remaining dumplings in the same way (using the remaining 4 tablespoons of oil and 1 extra cup of water).

Serve with chilli sauce, soy sauce or red vinegar for dipping.

Pleat one side of dough circle.

To prevent sticking, lift dumplings with spatula.

Makes 30
4 dried Chinese
   mushrooms
4 spring onions (scallions)
250 g (8 oz) minced
   (ground) pork
2 tablespoons finely
   chopped bamboo shoot
½ teaspoon finely grated
   fresh ginger
½ teaspoon salt

2 teaspoons light soy sauce
2 teaspoons sesame oil
2 teaspoons cornflour
   (cornstarch)
8 tablespoons peanut oil,
   for cooking
Dough:
2 cups (8 oz) plain
   (all-purpose) flour
1 cup boiling water

Cloud Swallows (Deep Fried Dumplings)

Place the mushrooms in hot water; soak for 30 minutes.

Drain the mushrooms, squeeze out excess moisture, trim off and discard the stems and chop the caps finely. Chop the prawns and spring onions. Combine mushrooms, prawns, spring onions, bamboo shoot, minced pork and seasonings; mix well together.

Put a small amount of filling (about ½ teaspoonful) in the centre of each wonton wrapper. Moisten the edges of the dough with water, fold over to a triangle with points slightly overlapping and press together. Then bring the two ends together, dab with a little of the filling mixture where they join and press to seal.

When all are made, deep fry a few at a time on medium heat until golden (about 2 minutes). Serve as an appetizer or as part of a meal with sweet and sour sauce.

Makes about 40
6 dried Chinese mushrooms
125 g (4 oz) raw prawns
4 spring onions (scallions)
3 tablespoons finely chopped bamboo shoot
250 g (8 oz) minced (ground) pork
1½ teaspoons salt
1 tablespoon light soy sauce
1 teaspoon sesame oil
250 g (8 oz) wonton wrappers
peanut oil for frying

Dried and soaked mushrooms.

Fold dough over filling into a triangle with overlapping points.

Join two ends of triangle together.

Spring Rolls

Cut pork into fine shreds.

Place filling at one end of each wrapper.

Roll wrapper, folding in ends to enclose filling

Traditionally eaten on New Year's Day and again in the spring, Spring Rolls (also known as Egg Rolls in America) can be easily made at home using the frozen wrappers which are available from Chinese stores and delicatessens.

SLICE THE PORK THINLY and then cut into fine shreds. Shell, de-vein and finely chop the prawns. Chop the water chestnuts and spring onions. Pinch the tails from the bean sprouts. Shred crisp leaf ribs of the cabbage to give 2 cups.

Heat a wok, add 1 tablespoon of peanut oil and fry the garlic and ginger over low heat until fragrant (do not brown). Add the pork, increase the heat and stir-fry until it changes colour. Add prawns and continue stirring until they are cooked. Remove from the wok to a large mixing bowl.

Heat the remaining tablespoon of peanut oil in the wok and fry the vegetables for 2 minutes. Add the sauces and salt. Make a space in the centre and stir in cornflour mixed with 1 tablespoon of cold water. Stir until the sauce boils and thickens. Remove from the wok to the pork-prawns mixture. Add the sesame oil and mix well. Allow to cool.

Put 2 tablespoons of the filling at one end of each spring roll wrapper and roll it up, turning in the ends so that the filling is completely enclosed. Dampen the edges with water and press to seal.

Heat plenty of oil in a wok and fry the spring rolls a few at a time until golden. Drain on absorbent paper, and serve immediately with chilli sauce.

Makes 20
250 g (8 oz) pork fillet
500 g (1 lb) raw prawns
12 water chestnuts
6 spring onions (scallions)
125 g (4 oz) bean sprouts
1 small Chinese cabbage
2 tablespoons peanut oil
½ teaspoon crushed garlic
½ teaspoon grated fresh ginger
1 tablespoon light soy sauce
1 tablespoon oyster sauce
1 teaspoon salt
3 teaspoons cornflour (cornstarch)
1 teaspoon sesame oil
1 packet frozen spring roll pastry, thawed in wrapping
peanut oil for deep frying

Shanghai Dumplings

Mix together the pork, salt, soy sauce, wine, finely chopped spring onions and grated ginger. Slowly beat in 3 tablespoons of water. This makes the filling juicy.

Measure flour into a bowl, make a well in the centre and pour in ½ cup (4 fl oz) cold water. Using the handle of a wooden spoon or chopsticks, mix to a dough, working from the centre and gradually incorporating the flour. Turn on to a lightly floured surface and knead for 5 to 6 minutes. The dough will become very smooth.

On the floured surface, roll the dough thinly and cut about 24 rounds 6 cm (2½ inches) in diameter. Place a small teaspoonful of the meat mixture in the centre of each round. Make two 'box pleats' on one side of the circle. Dampen the edges with water and seal them together to make dumplings.

Bring a large saucepan of water to the boil, add the dumplings and when they rise to the top and the water bubbles furiously, add 1 cup of cold water. Once more let the water bubble up, then add another cup of cold water. This keeps the dough firm and prevents bursting. Serve hot, with Chinese red vinegar and light soy sauce for dipping.

Makes about 24
300 g (10 oz) minced (ground) pork
½ teaspoon salt
1 teaspoon light soy sauce
1 teaspoon Chinese wine or dry sherry
2 spring onions (scallions)
½ teaspoon grated ginger
1½ cups (6 oz) flour
Chinese red vinegar for dipping
light soy sauce for dipping

Knead dough until very smooth.

Make two box pleats on one side of the dough circle.

Seal moistened edges to form dumpling.

Glazed Chicken Wings

Serves 4–6

750 g (1½ lb) chicken wings

3 spring onions (scallions), cut into 5 cm (2 inch) lengths

1 teaspoon grated fresh ginger

3 tablespoons Chinese wine or dry sherry

4 tablespoons dark soy sauce

2 teaspoons rock sugar, crushed

¼ teaspoon ground Szechwan pepper

1 tablespoon sesame oil

Remove the tips from the chicken wings and divide the wings at the joint. Put the wings into a saucepan of water to cover, and bring to the boil.

Drain, return the wings to the saucepan and add all other ingredients except sesame oil. Bring to the boil, then reduce the heat and simmer covered for 20 minutes, or until the chicken meat is tender. Turn the wings occasionally so that they are evenly coated with the sauce.

Remove the chicken wings to a plate. Reduce the sauce by cooking uncovered until thick. Turn off the heat, return the wings to the saucepan, sprinkle with the sesame oil and leave to cool. Serve at room temperature.

Remove tips from wings.

Divide chicken wings at joint.

Crush the rock sugar.

Steamed Egg Roll

Serves 8
Filling:
**185 g (6 oz) chicken, raw
prawns or lean pork**
½ teaspoon salt
2 teaspoons light soy sauce
½ teaspoon sesame oil
**1 teaspoon cornflour
(cornstarch)**
**1 tablespoon finely
chopped fresh coriander**
**1 tablespoon finely
chopped spring onion
(scallion)**
Wrappers:
5 eggs
½ teaspoon salt
1 tablespoon peanut oil
1 teaspoon sesame oil

Make a thin omelette, cook-ing on one side only.

Filling: Put the chicken, prawns or pork into an electric blender with salt, soy sauce and sesame oil and blend until smooth. Because the mixture is thick, it will be necessary to switch the blender on and off frequently and move the mixture on to the blades with a spatula. Then scrape it into a bowl and mix in the other ingredients, combining well. Alternatively, chop everything very, very finely with a sharp chopper until it has the consistency of a paste or use a food processor.

Wrappers: Beat the eggs well with salt. Reserve 1 table-spoon of beaten egg for sealing the egg rolls.

Heat a small omelette pan. Measure the peanut and sesame oils into a saucer. Dip a paper towel in the oil and grease the pan. Pour 2–3 tablespoons of egg mixture into the pan and make a thin omelette, cooking it on one side only; turn it on to a plate. Repeat with remaining egg mixture, greasing the pan each time. There will be 4 or 5 omelettes, depending on the size of your pan.

Divide the filling into the same number of portions as there are omelettes. Place each omelette on a board, cooked side up, and spread the filling almost to the edges using an oiled spatula or back of a spoon. Roll up like a Swiss roll and seal the edges with reserved beaten egg.

Lightly oil a plate with the mixed oils and place the rolls on it. Set the plate in a steamer (or on a rack in a saucepan of boiling water), cover and steam for 15 minutes. (The plate needs to be smaller than the steamer to allow steam to circulate.)

Remove from the steamer, allow to cool a little, then cut into slices diagonally. Serve hot or cold.

Spread filling on cooked side of omelette, almost to edges.

Place egg rolls on a plate in a steamer.

Bean Starch Sheets and Crystal Chicken

Wash the chicken breasts. In a pan that will be large enough to hold them in one layer, pour just enough water to almost cover the chicken pieces. Add ginger, spring onions and salt. Bring the water to the boil and then add the chicken pieces. Return to the boil, cover the pan, and cook for 3 minutes. Then turn the pieces over and cook for a further 3 minutes. Turn off the heat and allow to stand in the covered pan for 15 minutes. Remove the chicken pieces, allow them to cool, and then chill. (Save the chicken stock for another dish.)

Soak the sheets of green bean starch in hot water for 20 minutes. Then boil them for 5 minutes. Drain and refresh under cold running water. Cut into strips 5 cm (2 inches) × 1 cm (½ inch). Drain thoroughly and chill.

String the beans and cut them into diagonal strips. Drop them into boiling water to which has been added the peanut oil, and boil rapidly for 2 minutes. Drain and allow to cool.

Combine the sauce ingredients; in cold weather it may be necessary to warm the sesame paste to mix.

Remove the chicken meat from the bones and cut it into shreds. Arrange the strips of green bean starch on a platter, top with chicken meat and beans, and serve with the sauce spooned over. Serve on a bed of crisp lettuce leaves. If liked, garnish with fresh coriander.

Serves 4–6
4 half breasts of chicken
few slices of fresh ginger
2 spring onions (scallions)
½ teaspoon salt
3 sheets green bean starch
250 g (8 oz) French beans
1 tablespoon peanut oil
Sauce:
2 tablespoons Chinese sesame paste
1 tablespoon sesame oil
2 tablespoons dark soy sauce
2 tablespoons Chinese wine or dry sherry
1 tablespoon chilli sauce
1 tablespoon Chinese sweetened vinegar
2 teaspoons sugar

Sheets of green bean starch.

Cut the cooked green bean starch into strips.

Steamed Pearl Balls

Serves 6
1 cup (8 oz) uncooked rice
6 dried Chinese
   mushrooms
250 g (8 oz) minced lean
   steak
250 g (8 oz) minced pork
3 spring onions
   (scallions), finely
   chopped
½ teaspoon finely grated
   fresh ginger
½ teaspoon crushed garlic
1½ teaspoons salt
1 small egg, beaten
3 tablespoons finely
   chopped water
   chestnuts

Soak the rice in cold water to cover for at least 2 hours. Then drain well and spread it on paper towels to absorb excess water while preparing meatballs.

Soak the mushrooms in hot water for 30 minutes. Then squeeze out excess water, discard the stems and chop the caps finely. Put into a large bowl with all the remaining ingredients and mix very well with your hand so that the seasonings are evenly distributed. With wet hands shape into balls 2.5 cm (1 inch) in diameter.

Roll each ball separately in the rice, with enough pressure to make the rice stick and coat the ball.

Put the balls on a lightly oiled steamer rack or bamboo steamer, leaving a little space between because the rice will swell. Steam over fast boiling water for 30 to 35 minutes, adding more boiling water as water boils away. The rice swells and the balls will be covered with pearly grains when done. Serve with a dipping sauce of soy sauce flavoured with a few drops of chilli oil or sesame oil.

Note: If you do not have a steamer, improvise with a large pan that has a well-fitting lid. Put the pearl balls on a heatproof plate small enough to allow the steam to rise around it, and place the plate on a trivet or upturned bowl which will hold it above water level.

Roll meatballs in soaked rice.

Place in a lightly oiled steamer.

Cold Appetizer Platter

This consists of a selection of cold Chinese appetizers: Sweet Sour Gai Choy, Marinated Abalone, Steamed Chicken Pâté, Braised Mushrooms with Garlic and Barbecued Pork (see page 110). Serves 6.

Sweet Sour Gai Choy: Cut the gai choy (mustard cabbage) into chunks. Place the vinegar, salt and sugar in a saucepan, add 1½ cups (12 fl oz) water, and bring to the boil. Add oil, and boil the cabbage for 1 minute. Drain and chill.

Sweet Sour Gai Choy:
1 bunch gai choy (mustard cabbage)
½ cup (4 fl oz) vinegar
1 teaspoon salt
2 teaspoons sugar
1 tablespoon peanut oil

Cut the Gai Choy into chunks.

Marinated Abalone: Drain the abalone, cut into thin slices and place in a bowl. Combine the soy sauce, sugar, wine, sesame oil and ginger, pour it over the abalone and chill for 2 hours.

Drain the abalone and reserve the marinade to serve as a dip.

Marinated Abalone:
1 × 455 g (1 lb) can abalone
4 tablespoons light soy sauce
1 tablespoon sugar
1 tablespoon Chinese wine or dry sherry
1 tablespoon sesame oil
½ teaspoon finely grated fresh ginger

Cut abalone into thin slices.

Steamed Chicken Pâté: Skin and bone the chicken breast. Scrape the flesh to a purée using a sharp chopper (as described in the recipe for Chicken Velvet Fu Yung, on page 87), adding 2 teaspoons of water while puréeing. Alternatively grind finely in a food processor.

Mix in the salt, pepper, ginger, spring onions, coriander leaves, cornflour and egg white.

Lightly oil a bowl with peanut or sesame oil, and pack the chicken pâté into the bowl, smoothing the top. Place in a bamboo steamer or on a rack in a pan of boiling water and steam for 10 minutes or until set.

Allow to cool completely. Turn out of the bowl, cut in half, then slice each half neatly into even slices. Arrange on a serving platter.

Serve with a dipping sauce of 2 tablespoons of dark soy sauce mixed with ½ teaspoon of sesame oil.

Steamed Chicken Pâté:
375 g (12 oz) chicken breast
½ teaspoon salt
pinch of ground white pepper
¼ teaspoon finely grated fresh ginger
2 tablespoons finely chopped spring onions (scallions)
2 tablespoons finely chopped fresh coriander
1 teaspoon cornflour (cornstarch)
1 egg white, slightly beaten

Scrape the chicken flesh to a purée.

Braised Mushrooms with Garlic: Soak the mushrooms in 1½ cups of hot water for 30 minutes. Drain, and squeeze water from mushrooms (reserve the soaking liquid). Discard the stems.

Heat a wok, add peanut oil and when hot, fry the garlic and ginger until fragrant. Add mushroom caps and fry, pressing their undersides against the wok until they are golden brown.

Add the reserved mushroom liquid, the soy sauce, sugar and sesame oil. Cover with a lid, and simmer for 30 minutes or until liquid is absorbed and the mushrooms take on a shiny appearance.

Discard garlic and ginger, and serve mushrooms hot as an accompanying vegetable or cold as part of a cold appetizer selection.

Braised Mushrooms with Garlic:
30 g (1 oz) dried Chinese mushrooms
2 tablespoons peanut oil
1 large clove garlic, bruised
3 slices fresh ginger
2 tablespoons dark soy sauce
1 tablespoon sugar
2 teaspoons sesame oil

Press undersides of mushrooms against wok until golden.

Soups

In a Chinese meal, soup is not served at the beginning as in a western meal. For family meals, the soup is placed in the centre of the table together with the rice, and diners help themselves between other dishes. (This may explain why the Chinese table is always round.)

In a banquet, the soups (there is often more than one) are brought on as a change of pace between other courses. Some of the soups are light and clear, others are thick and robust in flavour. Some soups are prestige courses – intended to impress because of the rarity of ingredients and their cost. Shark fin soup and birds' nest soup fall into this category.

Soup is regarded as important nourishment for new mothers or invalids. Soup can also be a complete light meal when it is a noodle soup or one with dumplings, popularly known as long soup and short soup, respectively. Even the simplest soup should be based on strong stock that is home-made.

Stock

For chicken stock, use a chicken weighing about 1.5 kg (3 lb) and add 2 litres (8 cups) water, 3–4 thick slices of fresh ginger, 2–3 spring onions (scallions) and 2 teaspoons salt. The chicken should be stripped of extra fat near the tail, the tail removed and discarded. It is then jointed, and carefully washed to remove traces of internal organs and blood. To these basic ingredients I like to add a dozen or so whole black peppercorns and a small sprig of celery leaves, but these are optional. Bring to the boil, then reduce the heat to a gentle simmer, and skim the surface until the broth is clear. Cover and cook on very gentle heat for 2 hours or more.

If liked, and for reasons of economy, some of the chicken joints may be lifted out after they are just cooked, and used in another dish such as cold chicken with sesame sauce. For the same reasons of economy instead of using a whole chicken, the bones saved from preparing meat for other recipes may be collected and frozen; then when there is sufficient, stock may be made from them. Freeze stock in quantities suited to family requirements and there is always the basis of a good soup on hand.

After the stock has cooked, strain it and add salt to taste. A dash of dry sherry or Chinese wine may be added if liked. Chill and remove any fat from the surface, though a little fat may be left to give the soup more richness.

For a meat stock, use 1 kg (2 lb) meaty pork bones and proceed as for chicken stock, but use twice as much ginger and spring onions (scallions) to combat the stronger flavour of the meat. Chill, and remove fat from the surface.

Left: *clockwise from left: spring onions (scallions); straw mushrooms; eggs; soy sauce; bundles of egg noodles; chilli oil; carrot and Chinese cabbage, cut into lengths; wonton, ready to cook; Wonton Soup (see page 34); Long Soup with King Prawns (see page 37); bean starch noodles.*

Wonton Soup

Serves 6
125 g (4 oz) raw prawns
125 g (4 oz) minced
   (ground) pork
2 spring onions
   (scallions), finely
   chopped
½ teaspoon salt
1 tablespoon light soy
   sauce
¼ teaspoon crushed garlic
¼ teaspoon finely grated
   fresh ginger
125 g (4 oz) wonton
   wrappers
6 cups (1.5 litres) stock
3 tablespoons finely
   chopped fresh coriander
   or spring onions

In some restaurants this is known as 'Short Soup', the name referring to the dumplings as opposed to the long strands of noodles in 'Long Soup'.

SHELL AND DE-VEIN the prawns and chop them finely. Mix with the pork, spring onions, salt, soy sauce, garlic and ginger.

Place a scant teaspoon of the mixture on each square of wonton pastry. Moisten the edges, fold diagonally over the filling to make a triangle and press the edges together to seal. Moisten the two corners at the base of the triangle and join them together.

In a saucepan, bring a large amount of lightly salted water to a rolling boil and add a dash of oil. Drop in the dumplings, a few at a time, and after the water has returned to the boil, cook them for 5 minutes; add a small glass of cold water and bring to the boil again. Drain in a colander. Repeat until all dumplings are cooked.

Bring the stock to the boil, add the dumplings and return to the boil once more. Sprinkle with chopped coriander or spring onions, and serve hot.

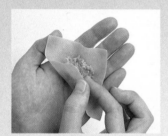

Fold pastry diagonally over filling and seal.

Fold corners across and seal.

Wonton ready to be cooked.

Szechwan Soup

This is a rich, robustly flavoured soup which is served in smaller than usual bowls.

SOAK THE MUSHROOMS in hot water for 30 minutes; then drain (reserve the liquid), discard the mushroom stems, and slice the mushroom caps finely. Soak the wood fungus in water for 10 minutes; then trim off any gritty portions and cut the fungus into small pieces. Soak noodles in hot water for 15 minutes, drain and cut into short lengths.

Heat the tablespoon of oil in a wok and fry the mushrooms and pork, stirring constantly, until they start to brown. Add the dark soy sauce, sugar and ½ cup (4 fl oz) of the mushroom water. Simmer, covered, until the mushrooms have absorbed almost all the liquid. Add prawns and bean curd, and stir-fry for 1 minute.

Bring the stock to a boil, add the noodles and return to the boil; simmer for 5 minutes. Add the light soy sauce, vinegar, wine, chilli oil and the fried mixture. Mix the cornflour smoothly with 2 tablespoons of cold water, and stir into the soup until it boils and thickens.

Dribble the beaten eggs into the simmering soup, stirring constantly so the egg separates into fine shreds. Season to taste with pepper and salt. Put a spoonful of wood fungus in each soup bowl and pour a ladle of the boiling soup over. Serve immediately.

Serves 6–8
8 dried Chinese mushrooms
1 tablespoon dried wood fungus
60 g (2 oz) bean thread noodles
1 tablespoon oil
½ cup finely chopped cooked pork
1 tablespoon dark soy sauce
2 teaspoons sugar
125 g (4 oz) chopped prawns
1 square fresh bean curd, diced
6 cups (1.5 litres) chicken or pork stock
1 tablespoon light soy sauce
1 tablespoon Chinese sweet vinegar
1 tablespoon Chinese wine or dry sherry
1 teaspoon chilli oil
1½ tablespoons cornflour (cornstarch)
2 eggs, beaten
salt and pepper to taste

Dried and soaked wood fungus.

Bean thread noodles.

Add the bean curd to the pork mixture.

Sung Dynasty Fish Soup

Gai Larn.

Cut the fish into paper thin slices.

Immerse the fish and broccoli in oil for 10 seconds.

Serves 4

3 dried Chinese
   mushrooms
125 g (4 oz) barramundi
   (sea bass) or rock cod
   fillets
2 stems Chinese broccoli
   (gai larn)
60 g (2 oz) barbecued pork
oil for deep frying
4 cups (1 litre) stock
1 tablespoon shao hsing
   wine or dry sherry
salt to taste
2 tablespoons cornflour
   (cornstarch) mixed with
   a little cold water
1 egg white, slightly
   beaten

Soak the mushrooms in hot water for 20 minutes. Discard the mushroom stems, and steam the mushroom caps for 15 minutes. Slice finely.

Cut the fish into paper-thin slices. Cut the stems of broccoli diagonally into very thin slices. Cut the barbecued pork into thin slices, then into small squares.

Heat the oil in a wok for deep frying and when very hot, immerse the fish and broccoli on a wire frying spoon for about 10 seconds only. This is long enough to cook both fish and broccoli if they are sliced thinly, and the quick heat turns the broccoli a vivid emerald green. Drain.

Heat the stock in a saucepan and when boiling, add wine, fish, broccoli, mushrooms and pork. Taste, and add salt if necessary. Add the cornflour mixture a little at a time, stirring constantly, until the soup is thick and clear.

Finally, dribble in the egg white which will set into shreds. The entire cooking process should take only a few minutes. Serve immediately.

Long Soup with King Prawns

Place the mushrooms in hot water; leave to soak for 30 minutes. Remove and discard the mushroom stems and slice the caps finely.

Shell and de-vein prawns, but leave the prawn tails on.

Soak the noodles in hot water to loosen the strands, then cook them just until tender in lightly salted boiling water. Rinse in cold water, and drain.

Bring the stock to the boil, add the shredded cabbage and the noodles and stir in sesame oil and salt to taste. Turn off the heat and leave while cooking the prawns.

Heat the peanut oil in a wok and gently fry the garlic and ginger for a few seconds. Add the prawns and toss on high heat, stirring constantly for 2 to 3 minutes or until they change colour. Add the sliced mushrooms and soy sauce, and stir. Remove from heat.

Ladle the hot noodle soup into individual bowls. Place a portion of prawns on top of each serving, and garnish with sprigs of fresh coriander if desired.

Serves 6
500 g (1 lb) large raw prawns
8 dried Chinese mushrooms
220 g (7 oz) fine egg noodles
6 cups (1.5 litres) prawn or chicken stock
salt to taste
¼ Chinese cabbage (wongah bak), shredded
1 teaspoon sesame oil
2 tablespoons peanut oil
½ teaspoon crushed garlic
½ teaspoon finely grated fresh ginger
1 tablespoon light soy sauce

Shred the wongah bak.

Loosen noodles while soaking so they cook evenly.

Pork and Prawn Ball Soup

Serves 6

Pork balls:

250 g (8 oz) minced (ground) pork

1/4 teaspoon finely grated fresh ginger

1/4 teaspoon crushed garlic

1/2 teaspoon salt

1 tablespoon finely chopped spring onion (scallion)

Prawn balls:

250 g (8 oz) raw prawns

1/4 teaspoon finely grated fresh ginger

1/4 teaspoon salt

1 slice soft white bread, crumbed

1 teaspoon cornflour (cornstarch)

Soup:

6 cups (1.5 litres) pork or chicken stock

1 tablespoon Chinese wine or dry sherry

1 tablespoon cornflour (cornstarch)

1/2 teaspoon sesame oil

2 tablespoons finely chopped spring onion (scallion)

Pork balls: Combine all ingredients, and form into balls the size of a large marble. Bring the stock to the boil, drop in the pork balls and return to the boil. Simmer for 15 minutes. Meanwhile make the prawn balls.

Prawn balls: Shell and de-vein the prawns and chop them very finely. Combine with all other ingredients, and form into balls the same size as the pork balls. Drop the prawn balls into the simmering stock after the pork balls have cooked for 15 minutes. Return to simmering point, cook for a further 3 minutes.

Stir in the wine, then the cornflour mixed with 1 tablespoon of cold water. Boil, stirring, until the soup is clear and slightly thickened (about 1 minute). Stir in the sesame oil and serve, garnished with the spring onion.

Combine ingredients for pork balls.

Roll into marble-sized balls.

Shrimp Velvet and Mushroom Soup

Wash and drain the shrimps. Remove shells and heads, but simmer these in the stock for extra flavour, strain.

Remove any sandy veins and chop the shrimps very finely until almost a purée, gradually adding a tablespoon of cold water while chopping. Blend the 3 teaspoons of cornflour with 1 tablespoon of cold water and the salt, then combine this with shrimp purée. Beat the egg whites until stiff and fold in. This may be done beforehand and the shrimp velvet refrigerated.

Drain the mushrooms and slice them. Combine the 1½ tablespoons of cornflour with the wine, soy sauce and sesame oil.

Bring the stock to the boil, add the sliced mushrooms and the cornflour mixture, and stir until the soup boils and thickens. Add the shrimp velvet and the frozen peas, and allow the soup to reach a gentle simmer once more. Taste and adjust seasoning if necessary; serve at once.

Serves 6
500 g (1 lb) raw shrimps (or prawns)
3 teaspoons cornflour (cornstarch)
1 teaspoon salt
3 egg whites
5 cups (1.25 litres) stock
1 small can straw mushrooms or champignons
additional 1½ tablespoons cornflour (cornstarch)
2 tablespoons Chinese wine or dry sherry
1 tablespoon light soy sauce
2 teaspoons sesame oil (optional)
3 tablespoons frozen peas

Chop shrimps until almost a purée.

Fold stiffly beaten egg whites into shrimp purée.

Shark Fin Soup

Slice chicken breast finely.

Add contents of the can of shark fin to stock.

Serves 6–8

6 dried Chinese mushrooms
1 large chicken breast
8 cups (2 litres) strong chicken stock
1 can shark fin
1 tablespoon light soy sauce
3 tablespoons Chinese wine or dry sherry
3 tablespoons cornflour (cornstarch)
1 egg, slightly beaten
2 thin slices cooked ham, cut into matchstick strips

Soak the mushrooms in hot water for 20 minutes. Discard the mushroom stems and slice the caps very thinly, then cut the slices into fine strips.

Skin and bone the chicken breast; slice it as finely as possible.

Bring the stock to the boil with the shark fin, soy sauce and Chinese wine. Add the mushrooms and chicken, and when it returns to the boil, stir in the cornflour mixed with 2 tablespoons of cold water. Cook, stirring, until it boils and thickens slightly. Dribble in beaten egg and stir so that the egg sets in fine shreds. Garnish the soup with ham, and serve at once.

Note: If preferred, substitute 250 g (8 oz) flaked crab-meat for the chicken.

Shanghai Egg Pouch Soup

Serves 6–8

125 g (4 oz) bean thread or cellophane noodles
6 dried Chinese mushrooms
half a Chinese cabbage (wongah bak)
8 cups (2 litres) chicken stock
Egg Pouches:
125 g (4 oz) minced (ground) pork
1 spring onion (scallion), finely chopped
¼ teaspoon finely grated fresh ginger
½ teaspoon salt
1 teaspoon cornflour (cornstarch)
3 eggs
pinch of salt

Swirl beaten egg in ladle over flame to coat evenly.

Fold one side of pouch over filling and seal.

This main-dish soup can be made more elaborate by adding slices of egg roll (page 27) or barbecued pork (page 110).

SOAK THE NOODLES in hot water for 20 minutes; then drain. Soak the mushrooms in hot water for 30 minutes; then drain, discard the stems and cut the caps into quarters. Wash the cabbage and cut it into thick slices.

To make the pouches: Combine the pork with the spring onion, ginger, salt and cornflour; mix well. In a separate bowl, beat the eggs with 1 tablespoon of cold water and a pinch of salt.

Lightly oil a ladle and hold it over low gas flame. Pour in about ¼ cup of the beaten egg, and swirl to give an even, thick coating of egg; pour excess egg back into the bowl. Put a teaspoon of the pork mixture on one side of the egg and fold the other side over, sealing the edge if necessary with a little of the uncooked egg. The pouches can be made in a heavy frying pan but the shape will not be as good. Place on a plate when made.

Cooking the soup: Heat the stock in a clay pot or flame-proof casserole, and season with salt if necessary. Add noodles, return to the boil and simmer for 5 minutes. Arrange the egg pouches in the pot and simmer for a further 5 minutes. In the centre place the sliced cabbage and the mushrooms, and give the soup a final 5 minutes' simmering.

Note: This dish can be prepared beforehand, to the stage where the noodles have been cooked in the soup. Have the egg pouches, cabbage and mushrooms ready in the refrigerator. About 20 minutes before serving, reheat the soup and continue with the recipe.

Crab and Corn Soup

Serves 6
250 g (8 oz) crabmeat,
   fresh or frozen
4 cups (1 litre) chicken
   stock
1½ tablespoons cornflour
   (cornstarch)
1 × 420 g (15 oz) can
   cream-style corn
1 tablespoon light soy
   sauce
2 tablespoons Chinese
   wine or dry sherry
salt and white pepper to
   taste
2 teaspoons sesame oil
2 tablespoons finely
   chopped spring onion
   (scallion)
2 tablespoons chopped
   fresh coriander leaves

Pick the crabmeat out of its shell if using fresh cooked crab, or thaw if using frozen crab. Flake the crabmeat and discard any bony pieces.

Bring the stock to the boil. Mix the cornflour smoothly with 2 tablespoons of cold water and stir this into the stock until it boils and thickens. Add the corn, soy sauce, wine, and salt and pepper to taste. Add the flaked crabmeat and heat through.

Turn off the heat and stir in the sesame oil. Sprinkle with chopped herbs, cover the pan with a lid for 1 minute, then serve.

Note: A variation is to use canned abalone instead of crab. Slice the abalone thinly, then shred it finely. Add it at the last minute, only heating through, because cooking can toughen it.

Flake the crabmeat and discard any bony pieces.

Duck and Lettuce Soup

Serves 4
4 cups (1 litre) duck stock
125 g (4 oz) diced cooked
   duck
salt to taste
1½ tablespoons cornflour
   (cornstarch)
half a small lettuce
1 spring onion (scallion)
2 teaspoons white vinegar
dash of chilli oil
   (optional)
1 teaspoon sesame oil
1 teaspoon Chinese wine
   or dry sherry

A well flavoured stock is essential for Chinese soups. Duck stock has a distinct flavour and is made by simmering the neck and carcase of duck in water with 2 or 3 slices of fresh ginger and a spring onion (scallion). This is simmered for about 2 hours to extract as much flavour as possible. Even the bones of cooked ducks can be used to make stock, which is then strained and can be frozen for future use.

BRING THE STOCK to the boil, add the cooked duck meat and salt to taste. Mix the cornflour smoothly with 1 tablespoon of cold water and stir this into the stock until it thickens slightly and becomes clear.

Shred the lettuce, first cutting it in two lengthways so that the shreds will not be inconveniently long. Slice the spring onion in fine diagonal slices.

Remove the soup from heat and add the lettuce, spring onion, vinegar and (optional) chilli oil. Taste for seasoning, and add salt if necessary. Cover the pan and leave for 2 minutes. Then stir in sesame oil and wine, and serve the soup at once.

Finely shred the lettuce.

Cut spring onions into fine diagonal slices.

Yunnan Pot Chicken Soup with Fuzzy Melon

Yunnan Pots are useful, decorative and not too expensive. Made from smooth red clay, the special feature is the narrow funnel which conducts steam up and into the pot. No liquid is added, but the dish makes its own strong, clear stock. Another version of this soup is made in a Chicken Pot—a covered pot with special base. Among those who can afford it, only the broth is used after prolonged steaming; the chicken pieces are discarded. SOAK THE MUSHROOMS in hot water for 30 minutes. Then squeeze out excess water, discard the stems, and cut the caps into halves or quarters. Rinse the chicken, cut off and discard the tail and excess fat. Cut the bird in half down the centre.

Remove thighs and drumsticks and pull off the skin. Chop the legs into 5 or 6 pieces, but do not cut through the joint. Remove the skin from the breast and cut each half of the breast into 4 pieces. Chop off wing tips (keep wing tips, neck and back for stock) and cut each wing into 3 pieces, again leaving the joint intact.

Put the chicken pieces into the pot and add ginger and spring onions. No water is needed in a Yunnan pot, but add a small amount (about 1 cup or 8 fl oz) to a pot that does not have a funnel.

Choose a saucepan just large enough to hold the Yunnan pot *above* water level when it has 5–7.5 cm (2–3 inches) of water in it. Bring to the boil and place the Yunnan pot on it. (If using the Chicken Pot or ordinary covered casserole, place in a large pan with hot water to come half-way up the casserole. Cover the pan with lid.)

Cook on medium high heat, keeping the water boiling briskly and adding more water as required, for 1½ to 2 hours.

Add peeled melon cut into chunky pieces, and cook for a further 10 minutes or until the melon is transparent. At the end of cooking, discard the spring onions and any large pieces of ginger. Stir in the wine, soy sauce, sesame oil and salt.

Serve the soup in the pot and accompany with steamed rice. Provide small individual sauce bowls for dipping the pieces of chicken in a flavouring sauce before eating.

Dipping Sauce: Mix equal parts of light soy sauce and Chinese wine or dry sherry with a few drops of sesame oil or a little finely grated fresh ginger, or toasted and crushed sesame seeds. For those who prefer a hot flavour, offer chilli sauce.

Serves 6
6 large dried mushrooms
1 × 1.5 kg (3 lb) roasting chicken
2 teaspoons shredded fresh ginger
2 spring onions (scallions)
250 g (8 oz) fuzzy melon or winter melon

2 tablespoons Chinese wine or sherry
1 tablespoon light soy sauce
½ teaspoon sesame oil
½ teaspoon salt

Chop chicken leg into 5 or 6 pieces.

The peeled fuzzy melon is cut into chunky pieces.

Mock Birds' Nest Soup

The dried fish maw.

Scrape chicken breast to a fine paste using cleaver.

Serves 6
30 g (1 oz) dried fish maw
1 chicken breast
2 egg whites
6 cups (1.5 litres) chicken
 stock
salt to taste
3 tablespoons cornflour
 (cornstarch)
3 tablespoons finely
 chopped water
 chestnuts
2 tablespoons finely
 chopped ham

Birds' nests are one of the luxury ingredients served at Chinese banquets and illustrate how prestigious foods are chosen, not for their flavour but for their rarity and high cost. Since these swifts' nests have to be gathered from high almost-inaccessible cliffs, they are both rare and expensive. They are almost without flavour, being spun by the bird from its own saliva, but since they contain predigested seaweed are probably nutritious. The little nests need careful cleaning to rid them of feathers and dirt, and all in all it is easier to get the banquet effect by substituting fish maw.

This may sound almost as weird, but is a fascinating ingredient to work with, being the lining of a fish's stomach which is thoroughly cleaned and dried, then deep fried so that it puffs up like a balloon. It has to be soaked and cut into fine shreds and has no fishy smell or taste—a good example of a texture ingredient. Since the flavours in this soup are so delicate, I suggest using a strong-flavoured ham such as prosciutto to add interest.

SOAK THE FISH maw in very hot water and put a weight on top to hold it down. When cool, squeeze out all the water and cut into fine shreds.

Remove skin and bones from the chicken breast, scrape to a fine paste, as in the recipe for Chicken Velvet Fu Yung (page 87), adding 2 tablespoons of cold water to lighten, then folding in the stiffly beaten egg whites.

Bring the chicken stock to a boil, add salt to taste. Add the shredded fish maw and simmer for 5 minutes. Mix the cornflour with 1 tablespoon of cold water to a smooth consistency and stir it into the stock until it thickens slightly and becomes clear. Add the water chestnuts. Stir in the chicken velvet, then remove from the heat. Ladle into a tureen, sprinkle the ham over, and serve.

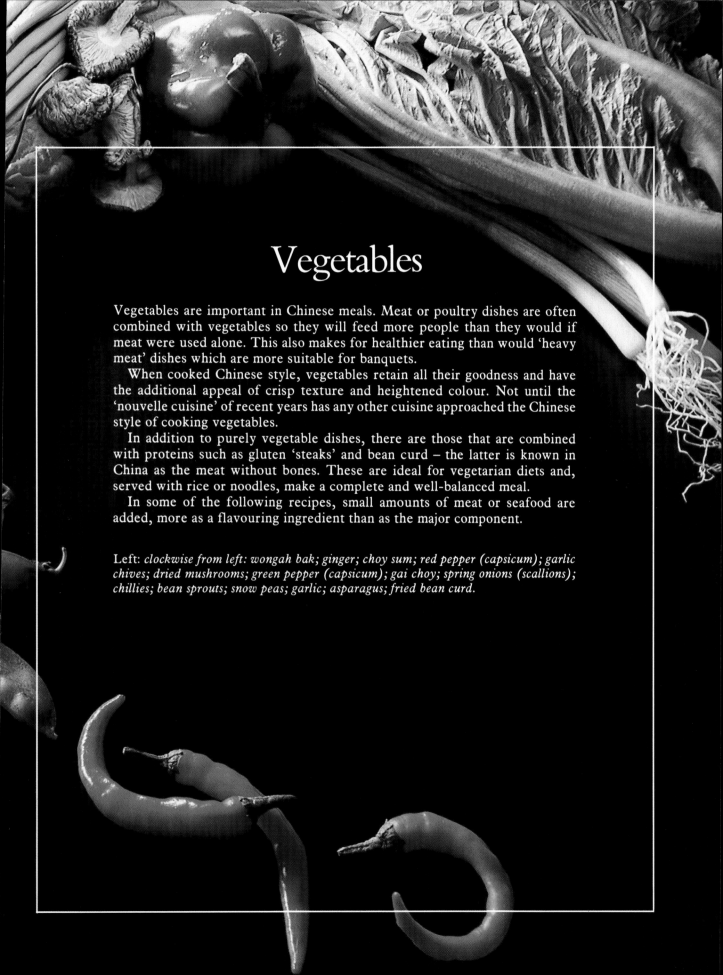

Vegetables

Vegetables are important in Chinese meals. Meat or poultry dishes are often combined with vegetables so they will feed more people than they would if meat were used alone. This also makes for healthier eating than would 'heavy meat' dishes which are more suitable for banquets.

When cooked Chinese style, vegetables retain all their goodness and have the additional appeal of crisp texture and heightened colour. Not until the 'nouvelle cuisine' of recent years has any other cuisine approached the Chinese style of cooking vegetables.

In addition to purely vegetable dishes, there are those that are combined with proteins such as gluten 'steaks' and bean curd – the latter is known in China as the meat without bones. These are ideal for vegetarian diets and, served with rice or noodles, make a complete and well-balanced meal.

In some of the following recipes, small amounts of meat or seafood are added, more as a flavouring ingredient than as the major component.

Left: *clockwise from left: wongah bak; ginger; choy sum; red pepper (capsicum); garlic chives; dried mushrooms; green pepper (capsicum); gai choy; spring onions (scallions); chillies; bean sprouts; snow peas; garlic; asparagus; fried bean curd.*

Asparagus in Oyster Sauce

Use the freshest asparagus for Chinese dishes. Tender asparagus spears will snap crisply if they are fresh. WASH THE ASPARAGUS spears, slice off and discard any tough ends. Bring plenty of water to boil in a wok. Add the oil and drop in the asparagus. Return the water to the boil and cook for 2 minutes, or until the asparagus spears are tender but still crisp.

Lift the asparagus out of the water on to a board and cut the spears into 5 cm (2 inch) lengths. Arrange on a serving dish.

Discard the asparagus cooking water. Put 3 tablespoons of cold water in the wok, stir in the oyster sauce and bring to the boil. Pour it over the asparagus and serve immediately.

Serves 4
2 bundles fresh asparagus
1 tablespoon peanut oil
1 tablespoon oyster sauce

Lower asparagus spears into rapidly boiling water.

Cut cooked asparagus into lengths.

Braised Chinese Cabbage

Trim the cabbage, discarding tough leaf portions, and cut into bite-size pieces. Heat the peanut oil, and fry the garlic and ginger for a few seconds, then add cabbage and stir-fry for 1 minute. Add the stock and sauce, cover and cook for 3 to 4 minutes, just until tender but still crisp. Stir in the cornflour, first mixed with 1 tablespoon cold water. Sprinkle with sesame oil, toss well and serve.

Cut cabbage into bite-sized pieces.

Serves 4
500 g (1 lb) Chinese cabbage (wongah bak), trimmed
3 tablespoons peanut oil
½ teaspoon crushed garlic
½ teaspoon finely grated fresh ginger
½ cup (4 fl oz) stock
1 tablespoon oyster sauce or light soy sauce
2 teaspoons cornflour (cornstarch)
1 teaspoon sesame oil

Add stock and sauce to lightly fried cabbage.

Braised Broccoli Stems

Peel the broccoli stems, cut them into bite-size lengths, and cut any thick stems in half. Bring lightly salted water to the boil in a saucepan, drop in the stems and return to the boil, then cook for 2 minutes or until bright green and just tender. (If using broccoli flowerheads as well, add them after removing the stems and give them no more than 1 minute's boiling.) Drain in a colander, but save ½ cup (4 fl oz) of the liquid.

Heat the peanut oil in a wok and stir-fry the broccoli and the ginger for 1 minute. Add the oyster sauce, soy sauce, sugar, sesame oil and cooking liqiud, and let it boil up. Mix the cornflour with 1 tablespoon of cold water and stir it into the liquid until it thickens slightly. Toss the broccoli pieces in the sauce and serve at once.

Serves 4

stems from a large bunch of broccoli
2 tablespoons peanut oil
½ teaspoon grated fresh ginger
1 tablespoon oyster sauce
1 tablespoon light soy sauce
1 teaspoon sugar
½ teaspoon sesame oil
liquid from blanching the broccoli
2 teaspoons cornflour (cornstarch)

Peel tough skin from broccoli stems.

Slice broccoli.

Stir-Fried Lettuce

Wash the lettuce, drain and dry well. Cut into halves lengthways, then cut each half twice lengthways and twice crossways to give chunky, bite-size pieces.

Heat a wok, add the peanut oil and swirl the wok to coat the inside with oil. Add the garlic and ginger and stir-fry for 10 seconds, then add the lettuce and stir-fry on high heat for 30 to 40 seconds. Turn off heat, add salt, sugar, soy sauce and sesame oil and toss to distribute the seasonings. The lettuce should retain its crisp texture. Serve at once, by itself or as a bed for other dishes.

Serves 4–6

1 firm lettuce
1–2 tablespoons peanut oil
½ teaspoon crushed garlic
¼ teaspoon finely grated fresh ginger
¼ teaspoon salt
1 teaspoon sugar
2 teaspoons light soy sauce
few drops of sesame oil

Cut halved lettuce into chunky pieces.

Braised Chinese Mushrooms and Bean Curd

Serves 4
**8 dried Chinese
  mushrooms**
**250 g (8 oz) fried bean
  curd or pressed bean
  curd**
2 tablespoons peanut oil
**2 spring onions
  (scallions), cut into
  5 cm (2 inch) lengths**
¾ cup (6 fl oz) stock
**1 tablespoon dark soy
  sauce**
1 tablespoon oyster sauce
½ teaspoon sugar
**1 teaspoon cornflour
  (cornstarch)**
1 teaspoon sesame oil

There are two types of bean curd suitable for this dish – pressed bean curd and squares of fried bean curd – both are available from Chinese stores. The pressed bean curd will require deep frying before adding to the sauce.

SOAK THE MUSHROOMS in water for 30 minutes. Drain, discard the mushroom stems and cut the caps in half.

Split squares of the fried bean curd into two, and then cut each square diagonally in half. If using the pressed bean curd, cut in the same way and then deep fry in hot oil until golden brown. Drain.

Heat a wok, add the peanut oil and swirl it around the wok. When hot, add the spring onions and mushrooms and stir on medium-high heat for about 30 seconds. Add the stock, soy sauce, oyster sauce, sugar and simmer, covered for 20 minutes. Add bean curd slices. Bring to the boil, cover the wok and simmer for 5 minutes.

Blend the cornflour with 1 tablespoon of water and stir it into the sauce until it boils and thickens. Add sesame oil, toss the mixture lightly, and serve.

Note: The soft white bean curd (tofu) available in packets can be used for this dish but take care to avoid mashing it. Cook the spring onions and mushrooms, add the liquids and seasonings, then simmer and thicken as described. At that stage, open the container, slide the bean curd on to a plate and drain off its liquid. Cut it into squares and carefully slide it into the sauce over a low heat. Do not stir, but spoon some of the sauce over the bean curd to heat it through. Slide the mixture out of the wok on to a serving dish.

The pressed bean curd (left) and fried bean curd.

Remove stems and halve mushroom caps.

Split squares of bean curd, then cut diagonally in half.

Capsicums with Pork and Prawns

Shell and de-vein the prawns; mince them finely. Combine them with the pork, salt, finely chopped spring onions and 2 teaspoons of the cornflour.

Cut the capsicums lengthways into quarters; discard the seeds and membranes, and wash them well. Cut each quarter capsicum across into half. Mound the minced mixture evenly on the capsicum pieces.

Blend the remaining 1 teaspoon of cornflour with 1 tablespoon of water. In a small bowl, combine the garlic, soy sauce, wine, bean sauce and sugar; mix in 5 tablespoons of water.

Heat 2 tablespoons of oil in a wok and fry half of the capsicum pieces, meat side down. When the filling is brown, turn them over and cook for a further 2 minutes. Remove to a plate. Add the remaining 2 tablespoons of oil to the wok and cook the remaining capsicums. Remove.

Pour the garlic-liquid mixture into the wok, stir until boiling, then thicken it with the blended cornflour. Return the capsicum and heat through. Scatter the matchstick strips of ham over the top, and serve.

Note: If the capsicums are large, cut them into 12 pieces instead of 8 so that the end result will be a convenient, bite-sized portion.

Serves 6

- 250 g (8 oz) green prawns
- 250 g (8 oz) minced (ground) pork
- 1 teaspoon salt
- 2 spring onions (scallions)
- 3 teaspoons cornflour (cornstarch)
- 3 medium-sized capsicums (red or green peppers)
- 1 teaspoon crushed garlic
- 1 tablespoon dark soy sauce
- 1 tablespoon Chinese wine or dry sherry
- 1 tablespoon bean sauce (Min Sze Jeung)
- 2 teaspoons sugar
- 4 tablespoons oil
- 30 g (1 oz) shoulder ham, cut into matchstick strips

Cut each capsicum into eight even-sized pieces.

Mound prawn and pork mixture on capsicum.

Fry capsicum, meat side down, then turn.

Stir-Fried Bok Choy

Serves 4–6
500 g (1 lb) bok choy
   (Chinese chard
   cabbage)
2 tablespoons peanut oil
1 clove garlic, bruised
   (optional)
3 slices fresh ginger
1 teaspoon sugar
1 teaspoon salt
1 teaspoon sesame oil

Prepare the bok choy. Separate the leaves from the heart, wash them well and trim off a small slice at their base. Lay the leaves flat on the chopping board and remove the tough leaf edges, leaving just a little border of green on the white stems. Cut the stems into 5 cm (2 inch) lengths.

Heat a wok, add the peanut oil and swirl to coat the wok. Add the garlic and ginger, and fry for a few seconds just until golden. Add the cabbage and stir-fry for 1 minute. Then add ¼ cup (2 fl oz) water and the sugar and salt; cover the wok and simmer for 2 minutes.

Uncover and stir-fry again until most of the liquid evaporates. Turn off the heat, sprinkle the sesame oil over, and toss to distribute the oil. Remove and discard the garlic and ginger. Serve at once, with other dishes.

Note: It the cabbage is not being served right away or must be reheated, use a slightly different method. After washing and cutting the stems, blanch them in a large pan of lightly salted boiling water with 1 tablespoon of oil added. Once the water returns to the boil, boil the cabbage for only 30 seconds, then drain. Just before serving stir-fry as above. This way the cabbage doesn't get that tired look if kept waiting.

Separate leaves of bok choy.

Remove the tough leaf edges.

To bruise garlic, hit firmly with chopper.

Shredded Gluten with Cashews

Serves 4
250 g (8 oz) prepared
    wheat gluten (see below)
250 g (8 oz) vegetables
3 tablespoons peanut oil
½ teaspoon grated fresh
    ginger
½ teaspoon crushed garlic
1 tablespoon bean sauce

½ teaspoon chilli sauce
    (optional)
1 tablespoon light soy
    sauce
2 teaspoons cornflour
    (cornstarch)
125 g (4 oz) deep fried
    cashew nuts

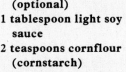

Shred the prepared gluten.

Choose a combination of two vegetables for this dish such as broccoli stems, red or green capsicum (red or green pepper), green beans, water chestnuts, bamboo shoots, spring onions (scallions).

PREPARE THE GLUTEN and after it has been boiled and cooled, cut it into shreds. Cut the vegetables the same size as the gluten.

Heat a wok, add 2 tablespoons of peanut oil and swirl to coat the inside of the wok. Cook the ginger and garlic over low heat for a few seconds. Then increase the heat, add the vegetables and stir-fry for a minute or two. Remove.

Add the remaining oil to the wok and stir-fry the gluten for 2 minutes. Mix the bean sauce, chilli and soy sauce with ½ cup (4 fl oz) water and stir it into the wok; cover the wok and simmer for 15 minutes.

Return the vegetables and cook for another 2 minutes. Blend cornflour with a little water, add and stir until the sauce boils and thickens. Add the cashews. Serve immediately with hot rice.

PREPARATION OF GLUTEN 'STEAKS': In Oriental vegetarian diets we find soybeans in various forms, especially bean curd which the Chinese call 'the meat without a bone' because of its high protein value. Another way of introducing protein is with the gluten 'steaks'. Gluten is the protein part of wheat and gluten flour may be purchased from health food stores. The spongy steaks can be sliced or shredded as required and they absorb flavours readily.

Yields about 300 g (10 oz)
prepared gluten
½ cup (3 oz) gluten flour
½ cup (4 fl oz) water

PUT THE GLUTEN FLOUR and water into a bowl and mix with a wooden spoon. It may be necessary to add a little more water, because the absorbency varies (as it does with plain flour). It will form a rubbery dough. With wet hands, shape the dough into a ball, place it in a bowl, cover and leave for 30 minutes.

Bring a large saucepan of water to the boil. On a wet board, cut the dough with a wet knife into slices 1.5 cm (¾ inch) thick. Drop them into the boiling water, cover the saucepan and cook for 30 minutes. They will swell to about three times their size.

Drain in a colander and allow to cool. When cool enough to handle, squeeze gently to remove excess water. Refrigerate, covered with plastic wrap. They will keep for up to a week.

Pickled Mustard Cabbage

Put the sugar, water, salt and vinegar into a saucepan and stir over heat until the sugar dissolves. Bring to the boil and simmer for 5 minutes. Leave to cool completely.

Using only the stem and leaf ribs of the well-washed mustard cabbage, cut into chunks 2.5 cm (1 inch) long. After trimming there should be 250 g (8 oz). (The leaves may be shredded and used in soup or other dishes.)

Bring a large saucepan of water to the boil and blanch the mustard cabbage chunks for 1 minute. Drain, and cool under running cold water.

Rinse out a large glass jar with hot water, put in the mustard cabbage and ginger. Top up with the spiced vinegar mixture, cover and refrigerate for 3 to 4 days before using.

This crisp pickled vegetable makes a refreshing snack, and the flavour is enhanced when eaten with a little sesame oil.

1 cup (8 oz) sugar
3 cups (24 fl oz) water
1 tablespoon salt
²/₃ cup (5½ fl oz) cider vinegar
1 bunch 500 g (1 lb) mustard cabbage (gai choy)
4 slices of fresh ginger

The mustard cabbage.

Drain and cool the blanched cabbage.

Pickled Vegetables

1 small white turnip
½ cucumber
½ carrot
10 slices fresh ginger
1 red chilli, diced

1 red capsicum (red pepper), diced
1 tablespoon salt
4 tablespoons sugar
4 tablespoons vinegar

Cut the turnip, cucumber and carrot into bite-sized pieces (equal to about 2 cups). Add the ginger slices, red chilli, red capsicum and salt. Mix well, and leave to stand for 6 hours.

Lightly rinse the vegetables, drain, then return them to a bowl. Add sugar and vinegar, mix well and allow to stand for 6 hours in the refrigerator.

Note: The ingredients may be diced, shredded or diagonally cross-cut into big or little pieces according to your preference, and the soaking time should be adjusted accordingly.

Cut vegetables into bite-sized pieces.

Add ginger, chilli, capsicum and salt to vegetables.

Eggplant, Szechwan Style

Slice off and discard the stalk end of the eggplants, but do not peel them. Cut in half lengthways, then into wedges lengthways each about 2.5 cm (1 inch) thick. Cut the wedges into 5 cm (2 inch) lengths.

Heat the peanut oil in a wok or frying pan, and fry half of the pieces of eggplant at a time on high heat, turning the pieces so that they are evenly browned. Let them cook to a dark golden brown, then lift them out with a slotted spoon and drain on absorbent paper. When all the eggplant pieces have been fried, set them aside to cool. The oil that remains may be strained and used again.

Combine the sauce ingredients and stir until sugar dissolves.

Pour off all but 1 tablespoon of oil remaining in the pan. Heat, then add the ginger and garlic and stir quickly over medium heat until they turn golden.

Add the sauce mixture, bring to the boil, then return the eggplant and cook over high heat, turning the eggplant pieces over until most of the sauce is absorbed. Transfer to a serving dish as soon as cooking is completed (don't leave eggplant in the wok or a metallic taste will develop). Serve warm or cold.

Serves 6
2 eggplants about 500 g
   (1 lb) each, or 1 kg (2 lb)
   smaller eggplants
2 cups (16 fl oz) peanut oil
1 teaspoon finely grated
   ginger
1 teaspoon finely chopped
   garlic
Sauce:
4 tablespoons dark soy
   sauce
2 tablespoons vinegar
1 tablespoon Chinese wine
   or dry sherry
2 tablespoons sugar
1 teaspoon sesame oil
1 teaspoon chilli oil
   (optional)
1–2 teaspoons sweet chilli
   sauce

Cut wedges of eggplant into lengths.

Deep-fry eggplant in two lots until brown, then drain.

Stir-Fried Watercress with Bean Curd

Serves 4
500 g (1 lb) watercress
1 teaspoon salt
2 tablespoons peanut oil
1 large dried red chilli
½ teaspoon crushed garlic
2 teaspoons sesame oil
250 g (8 oz) fresh bean curd
Sauce:
1 tablespoon light soy sauce
1 tablespoon Chinese wine or dry sherry
½ teaspoon sesame oil
1 teaspoon chopped fresh coriander leaves

Wash the watercress well and shake dry. Finely chop the leaves and stems, place in a bowl, sprinkle with the salt and toss well. Cover the bowl and chill for 30 minutes or longer. Drain and squeeze out liquid.

Heat a wok over a medium heat, add the peanut oil and when hot, add the whole chilli and fry until it is dark in colour. On high heat fry the garlic for just 3 or 4 seconds; add the watercress and stir-fry, turning constantly for 30 seconds. Turn off the heat, mix in the sesame oil and turn the mixture out into a serving dish. Allow to cool, and chill.

Have the bean curd well chilled. Combine the ingredients for the sauce in a small serving bowl. Drain the bean curd, cut it into squares and carefully place them on the chilled watercress. Sprinkle the sauce over the dish.

Finely chop leaves and stems of washed watercress.

A whole chilli is fried in the oil for flavour.

Carefully cut the drained bean curd into slices.

Vegetable Platter with Sesame Sauce

Serves 6
30 g (1 oz) agar-agar
**250 g (8 oz) button
mushrooms**
2 tablespoons peanut oil
salt to taste
250 g (8 oz) green beans
4 spring onions (scallions)
250 g (8 oz) bean curd
1 carrot
Sesame Sauce:
**3 tablespoons bottled
sesame sauce**
**2 tablespoons light soy
sauce**
2 tablespoons water
2 tablespoons sesame oil
1/2 teaspoon chilli oil

This cold vegetable platter makes an ideal hors d'oeuvre or a light meal. Other suitable vegetables are cooked asparagus, blanched broccoli stems, sliced (canned) water chestnuts, strips of zucchini (courgettes) that have been briefly fried in a little oil, and cold cooked egg noodles.
SOAK THE AGAR-AGAR in cold water for 10 minutes; then drain and cut into 5 cm (2 inch) lengths. Wipe the mushrooms with a damp towel, discard their stems and slice the caps.

Heat a wok, add the peanut oil and heat. Add the mushrooms and stir-fry over a moderate heat for 2 minutes. Turn out on to a serving dish and season to taste with salt. Allow to cool.

String the beans, removing ends; leave whole, or halve if large. Blanch the beans in boiling water for 3 minutes, then drain and cool. Cut the spring onions into bite-size lengths. Slice the bean curd. Peel the carrot and cut it into strips. Blanch briefly – they should still be crisp.

Arrange the vegetables on a serving platter, with a bowl of the sauce for spooning over them.
Sesame Sauce: Stir the sesame sauce until it is smooth, then blend in the other ingredients. In cold weather it may be necessary to warm the sesame sauce before mixing.

The dried and soaked agar-agar.

Slice mushroom caps.

Stir-Fried Eggs with Mixed Vegetables

Serves 4–6
4 eggs
½ teaspoon salt
15 g (1 oz) dried wood fungus
250 g Chinese cabbage
1 carrot
4 spring onions (scallions)
2 tablespoons peanut oil
½ teaspoon finely grated fresh ginger
1 tablespoon light soy sauce
½ teaspoon sugar
1 teaspoon sesame oil

Wood fungus is a texture ingredient which looks rather pretty when it is soaked and swells into shapes like billowing storm clouds. It is also known as cloud ear fungus or wun yee.

BEAT THE EGGS with salt until yolks and whites are mixed.

Soak the wood fungus in a large bowl of water for 15 minutes. Then rinse well and trim off any gritty portions. Cut large pieces in half.

Cut cabbage leaves in half lengthways (or thirds if they are large), then shred finely crossways. This keeps the shreds from being long and stringy. Cut the carrot into matchstick strips. Cut the spring onions into short lengths.

Heat a wok, add 1 tablespoon of the peanut oil and stir-fry the eggs until they set. Remove to a plate.

Wipe out the wok. Add the remaining tablespoon of peanut oil and when hot, fry the ginger for a few seconds. Add the cabbage and carrot, and stir-fry for 1 minute, then cover the wok and cook until half tender (about 2 minutes). Add the spring onions, wood fungus, soy sauce, sugar and sesame oil. Stir to mix, cover the wok and cook on low heat for 1 minute. Add the cooked eggs, toss well together, and serve immediately.

Finely shred the cabbage.

Stir-fry beaten eggs until they set.

Add spring onions and wood fungus to vegetables in wok.

Stir-Fried Salad Sprouts

Serves 4

3 cups salad sprouts (mung bean, alfalfa, fenugreek, lentil)
1 large carrot
2 spring onions (scallions)
stalks of choy sum (optional)
1 tablespoon peanut oil
½ teaspoon finely chopped garlic
1 tablespoon light soy sauce
1 tablespoon oyster sauce
few drops of sesame oil

Rinse the salad sprouts in a large bowl of cold water. Drain well in a colander. Pinch off straggly tails of the bean sprouts if time permits.

Cut the carrot into long diagonal slices no more than 6 mm (¼ inch) thick; then stack three or four slices together and cut into matchstick strips. Either blanch the carrot strips in boiling water for 1 minute; or if you have a microwave cooker, cover them with plastic wrap and microwave for 30 seconds.

Cut the lower half of the spring onions into bite-size lengths; roughly chop the dark green leaves (keep the two separate). If using choy sum, cut into bite-size lengths.

Place a wok over heat and when hot, pour in the peanut oil and allow to heat, then swirl the wok so that it is coated with oil. Throw in the garlic and spring onion leaves, and stir-fry for 30 seconds. Add the choy sum, and stir-fry for 1 minute. Add the well-drained sprouts, white portion of spring onion and carrot, and stir-fry for 1 minute. Then add the soy sauce and oyster sauce, and mix well. Turn off the heat, sprinkle the sesame oil over, toss to mix, and serve at once.

Note: If liked, bean curd (cut into strips or dice) may be added with the sprouts. In a vegetarian diet, this provides protein.

Rinse and drain the combined sprouts.

Cut carrots into matchstick strips.

Chop tops of spring onions and cut white part into lengths.

Braised Gluten with Vegetables

Thinly slice the gluten.

Discard any hard bits from soaked wood fungus.

Add mushroom liquid and flavourings to fried gluten.

Prepare the gluten and after it has been boiled and cooled, cut it into thin slices.

Soak the mushrooms in 1½ cups (12 fl oz) hot water for 20 minutes. Drain (reserving the water), discard the mushroom stems and cut the caps into slices. Soak the wood fungus in cold water for 10 minutes; drain, discard any hard bits and cut into bite-size pieces.

Cut the carrot into matchstick strips. Cut the beans into diagonal slices. Chop the spring onions and put them on a saucer with the grated ginger.

Heat a wok, add the peanut oil and swirl to coat the wok. Fry the spring onions and ginger for a few seconds; then add the sliced gluten and mushrooms and fry for a minute or two. Add 1 cup of the mushroom soaking liquid and stir in the soy sauces, sugar and 2 teaspoons of the sesame oil. Cover and simmer on low heat for 8 minutes.

Add the carrots and beans, cover the wok and simmer for a further 8 minutes.

Finally, stir the wood fungus through and cook for 2 minutes longer. The liquid in the wok should now be reduced to about ¼ cup. Sprinkle with the remaining teaspoon of sesame oil, and serve at once.

Serves 4

250 g (8 oz) prepared
   gluten (see page 53)
6 dried Chinese
   mushrooms
2 tablespoons dried wood
   fungus
1 carrot
12 green beans
3 spring onions (scallions)
1 teaspoon finely grated
   ginger
2 tablespoons peanut oil
1 tablespoon light soy
   sauce
1 tablespoon dark soy
   sauce
2 teaspoons sugar
3 teaspoons sesame oil

Bean Curd with Hot Sauce

Cut the bean curd into small dice. Have the chopped ginger, garlic and spring onion ready on a plate. Bring 1 litre of water to a rolling boil in a wok, add the diced bean curd and bring the water back to the boil for a few minutes until the bean curd is heated through. Pour into a sieve and allow to drain.

Dry off the wok, add the peanut oil and when hot, stir-fry the ginger, garlic and spring onion.

Add the stock (or water), bean sauce, chilli paste, tomato sauce, salt, sugar and soy sauce; allow it to boil. Blend the cornflour with 1 tablespoon of cold water, and stir it into the mixture.

Place the bean curd in the wok, and sprinkle the sesame oil over. With a large ladle, scoop the sauce over it – taking care not to mash the bean curd. If liked serve on a bed of Stir-Fried Lettuce (see page 49) and garnish with a chilli flower.

Cut bean curd into dice.

Scoop sauce over bean curd.

Serves 4

- 4 squares pressed bean curd
- 1 teaspoon finely chopped ginger
- 1 teaspoon finely chopped garlic
- 1 tablespoon finely chopped spring onion (scallion)
- 1 tablespoon peanut oil
- 1/2 cup (4 fl oz) stock or water
- 1 teaspoon ground bean sauce (mor sze jeung)
- 1 teaspoon chilli paste
- 1 tablespoon tomato sauce
- 1/2 teaspoon salt
- 1/2 teaspoon sugar
- 1 teaspoon dark soy sauce
- 1 teaspoon cornflour (cornstarch)
- drops of sesame oil

Braised Bitter Melon

Serves 4–6

3 medium-sized bitter
  melons
375 g (12 oz) minced
  (ground) pork, or raw
  prawns
2 tablespoons finely
  chopped spring onions
  (scallions)
1 teaspoon finely grated
  fresh ginger
½ teaspoon crushed garlic
½ teaspoon salt
1 egg, beaten
3 teaspoons cornflour
  (cornstarch)
1 tablespoon canned
  salted black beans
1 teaspoon finely chopped
  garlic
4 tablespoons peanut oil
1 teaspoon sesame oil
Sauce
½ cup (4 fl oz) stock or
  water
1 tablespoon light soy
  sauce
1 teaspoon sugar

Cut each bitter melon crossways into 4 cm (1½ inch) slices, discarding stem end and pointed tip. With a sharp knife, remove and discard the spongy centre and seeds, leaving tubular sections.

Mix pork or prawns with ginger, crushed garlic, salt, 2 tablespoons of the beaten egg and 2 teaspoons of the cornflour, combining thoroughly. Fill the sections of melon with this mixture, mounding the filling slightly on one side.

Rinse the black beans in a strainer under cold water, drain well, and mash the beans with a fork or chop finely. Mix with the finely chopped garlic. In a separate bowl, mix the sauce ingredients together.

Heat a wok, add the peanut oil and swirl to coat. Put the pieces of melon into the wok and fry on medium heat just until the filling starts to brown. This may be done in batches. Lift out on a slotted spoon and set aside on a plate.

Pour off all but a tablespoon of oil, add the black beans-garlic mixture and fry, stirring, for 1 minute. Add the sauce ingredients mixed together and bring to the boil. Return slices of melon to the wok with the rounded side upwards. Cover the wok and simmer on low heat for 15 to 20 minutes.

Remove the melon pieces to a serving plate. Mix the remaining teaspoon of cornflour with 1 tablespoon of cold water, add it to the sauce in the wok and stir until it thickens. Drizzle in the remaining beaten egg, stirring as it sets. Turn off heat and stir in sesame oil. Pour over the melon and serve with rice.

Remove spongy centre from thick slices of bitter melon.

Fill bitter melon with pork mixture.

Fry pieces of melon until filling begins to brown.

Stir-Fried Long Beans and Minced Pork

Serves 4–6

500 g (1 lb) long beans
3 tablespoons peanut oil
3 teaspoons finely grated
   fresh ginger
250 g (8 oz) minced
   (ground) pork
3 tablespoons roughly
   chopped spring onions
   (scallions)

Sauce:
½ cup (4 fl oz) chicken
   stock
1 tablespoon light soy
   sauce
2 teaspoons oyster sauce
1 teaspoon cornflour
   (cornstarch)

Top and tail the long beans, wash and pat dry on paper towels. Cut into 5 cm (2 inch) lengths and set aside.

Mix the sauce ingredients except for cornflour; set aside. Separately, mix the cornflour with 1 tablespoon of cold water; set this aside as well.

Heat a wok, add 2 tablespoons of the oil and swirl. Fry 1 teaspoon of the ginger for 10 seconds, then add the beans and stir-fry for 1 minute. Remove to a plate.

Return the wok to the heat, add the remaining tablespoon of oil and when hot, add the remaining 2 teaspoons of ginger, fry for a few seconds, then add the pork and stir-fry on high heat until its colour changes. Keep tossing, and press against the hot wok with back of frying spoon so that it is all well cooked.

Add the sauce ingredients and the beans, stir, cover, and cook for 3 minutes. Uncover, add spring onions and toss over high heat. Stir in the cornflour-water paste until the sauce thickens. Serve immediately.

Cut long beans into lengths.

Stir-fry pork until colour changes.

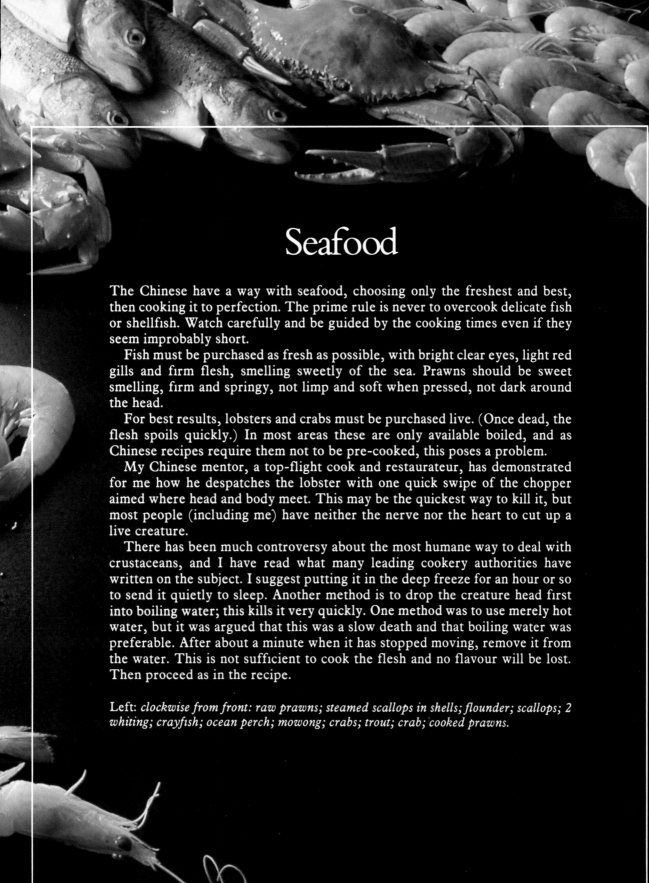

Seafood

The Chinese have a way with seafood, choosing only the freshest and best, then cooking it to perfection. The prime rule is never to overcook delicate fish or shellfish. Watch carefully and be guided by the cooking times even if they seem improbably short.

Fish must be purchased as fresh as possible, with bright clear eyes, light red gills and firm flesh, smelling sweetly of the sea. Prawns should be sweet smelling, firm and springy, not limp and soft when pressed, not dark around the head.

For best results, lobsters and crabs must be purchased live. (Once dead, the flesh spoils quickly.) In most areas these are only available boiled, and as Chinese recipes require them not to be pre-cooked, this poses a problem.

My Chinese mentor, a top-flight cook and restaurateur, has demonstrated for me how he despatches the lobster with one quick swipe of the chopper aimed where head and body meet. This may be the quickest way to kill it, but most people (including me) have neither the nerve nor the heart to cut up a live creature.

There has been much controversy about the most humane way to deal with crustaceans, and I have read what many leading cookery authorities have written on the subject. I suggest putting it in the deep freeze for an hour or so to send it quietly to sleep. Another method is to drop the creature head first into boiling water; this kills it very quickly. One method was to use merely hot water, but it was argued that this was a slow death and that boiling water was preferable. After about a minute when it has stopped moving, remove it from the water. This is not sufficient to cook the flesh and no flavour will be lost. Then proceed as in the recipe.

Left: clockwise from front: raw prawns; steamed scallops in shells; flounder; scallops; 2 whiting; crayfish; ocean perch; mowong; crabs; trout; crab; cooked prawns.

Fried Fish with Chilli Bean Sauce

Scale and clean the fish thoroughly, leaving head and tail on. Trim off any spines with kitchen scissors. Wash fish well and dry on paper towels. With a sharp knife or chopper, score the fish lengthways, making parallel cuts about a finger's width apart and almost through to the bone to allow seasonings to penetrate.

Combine 2 tablespoons of the wine with the light soy sauce, and marinate the fish in this mixture, making sure it goes into all the cuts.

Drain the marinade from the fish. Heat a wok, add the peanut oil and when very hot, add the fish. Deep-fry for 3 to 4 minutes on each side until both fish are brown and cooked. Turn the fish once only when cooking. Drain on a slotted spoon and place the fish on a heated serving platter.

Pour off most of the oil from the wok but leave about 3 tablespoons. Stir-fry the ginger and garlic over medium heat until the garlic starts to turn golden. Add the bean sauce, and stir; then add 1 cup (8 fl oz) water.

Mix the sauce ingredients with 1 tablespoon of cold water; add this to the wok and stir constantly until the mixture comes to the boil and thickens slightly. Finely chop the spring onions and stir them in. Pour the sauce over the fish and serve with rice.

Score fish lengthways.

Deep fry fish, turning once.

Serves 4
**2 whole firm white fish,
    about 750 g (1½ lb) each**
**4 tablespoons Chinese
    wine or dry sherry**
**2 tablespoons light soy
    sauce**
peanut oil for frying
**1 tablespoon finely grated
    ginger**

2 teaspoons crushed garlic
**2 tablespoons hot bean
    sauce**
4 spring onions (scallions)
Sauce:
**2 teaspoons cornflour
    (cornstarch)**
1 teaspoon sugar
**2 tablespoons dark soy
    sauce**

Fried Mountain Trout with Ginger

Clean the cavity of the trout with damp kitchen paper dipped in salt. Make shallow diagonal cuts on the fish and rub in salt and five spice powder mixed together. Roll the fish in cornflour to coat it and dust off any excess.

Cut the spring onions in bite-size pieces. Combine the sauce ingredients.

Heat a wok, add the peanut oil and when very hot, fry the ginger and spring onions for just a few seconds until they are soft but not brown. Remove on a frying spoon and set aside on a plate. Place the fish in the wok, and fry until they are golden brown underneath; then turn them over, lower the heat and fry until the other side is browned too and the fish are cooked through.

Pour off as much oil as possible. Pour the sauce mixture over the fish. Return the ginger and spring onions, raise the heat and cook for 1 minute or until the sauce boils. Lift the fish on to a warm serving dish, spoon the sauce over, and serve garnished with coriander and carrots.

Note: Young tender ginger, which has translucent skin and pink tips, is best for this dish. If this is not available, reduce the quantity of ginger by half.

Serves 4

4 trout, about 185 g (6 oz) each
1 teaspoon salt
½ teaspoon five spice powder
3 tablespoons cornflour (cornstarch)
3 spring onions (scallions)
6 tablespoons peanut oil
2 tablespoons very finely shredded ginger

Sauce:
2 tablespoons Chinese red vinegar or wine vinegar
2 tablespoons Chinese wine or sherry
3 tablespoons light soy sauce
2 teaspoons sugar
2 teaspoons sesame oil
2 tablespoons chopped fresh coriander

Finely shred young ginger.

Fry the fish in wok, turning once.

Return ginger and spring onion to fish and sauce.

Crisp-Skin Fish with Mushroom Sauce

Serves 4–6

1 whole fish, about 1.5 kg (3 lb) – snapper, bream, or other firm white fish

flour, seasoned with salt

oil for frying

1 large lemon for garnishing

Mushroom Sauce:

6 dried Chinese mushrooms

6 tablespoons vinegar

6 tablespoons sugar

2 tablespoons light soy sauce

2 tablespoons finely chopped spring onion (scallion)

1 tablespoon cornflour (cornstarch)

2 tablespoons preserved cucumber slices in syrup (optional)

Buy the fish cleaned and scaled, but with the head left on. Trim the fins and tail with kitchen scissors, and wipe out the cavity with paper towels dipped in coarse salt. Wash well and dry thoroughly. With a sharp knife, slash the fish diagonally on each side almost to the centre bone, forming diamond shapes in the flesh. Set the fish aside while you make the sauce.

Mushroom Sauce: Soak the mushrooms in hot water for 30 minutes. Drain, discard the mushroom stems and slice the caps finely. Put the mushrooms, vinegar, sugar and soy sauce into a small saucepan; add ¾ cup (6 fl oz) water, and boil for 5 minutes. Add the spring onion. Add the cornflour blended with 1 tablespoon of cold water and cook, stirring, until the sauce is clear and thickened. Remove from heat and keep warm. Stir in the preserved cucumber.

Dip the fish in seasoned flour, shaking off excess. Deep fry the fish in hot oil until golden brown. Drain it on a wire spoon and transfer it to a serving dish. Spoon the sauce over and garnish with lemon butterflies. This fish is good hot or cold.

Score the fish into a diamond pattern.

Add preserved cucumber to sauce.

Fish Braised in Soy Sauce

Serves 4–6

1 whole fish, about 1.5 kg
   (3 lb)
1 teaspoon salt
2 tablespoons cornflour
   (cornstarch)
1 teaspoon five spice
   powder
2 spring onions (scallions)
6 tablespoons peanut oil
6 thin slices fresh ginger
2 cloves garlic, bruised
1 whole star anise
Sauce:
4 tablespoons dark soy
   sauce
2 tablespoons dry sherry
2 teaspoons sesame oil
1 tablespoon sugar

Wash and clean the fish, leaving the head on. Wipe dry with paper towels. Score the fish lightly, no more than half-way to the bone, making three or four diagonal slashes on each side. Combine salt, cornflour and five spice powder; rub this mixture over the fish to coat it lightly, dust off excess.

Cut the spring onions into short lengths. In a bowl, combine the sauce ingredients with ½ cup (4 fl oz) water, and stir until the sugar dissolves.

Heat a wok, add the peanut oil and when very hot, slide the fish very carefully into the oil; fry over high heat for 2 minutes or until the underside of the fish is golden brown. Turn the fish, using a large spatula under the thickest part of the fish and helping it with a second spatula. Cook on the second side for a further 2 minutes or until golden.

Pour off the oil. Add the sauce mixture, pouring it over the fish. Add the spring onions, ginger, garlic and star anise. Reduce the heat so that the liquid simmers gently; cover the wok and cook for 10 to 12 minutes, basting two or three times with the sauce. Test at thickest part of fish with point of knife – if the flesh is milky white and flakes easily, the fish is cooked.

Carefully lift fish on to serving plate and spoon some sauce over it.

Rub salt, cornflour, and five spice powder into the scored fish.

Add spring onions, ginger, garlic and star anise to fish in wok.

Braised Rainbow Trout in Piquant Sauce

Score fish on both sides.

Fry fish in hot oil.

Simmer fish in sauce.

Serves 4–6
**1 rainbow trout, about 1 kg
   (2 lb)**
**2 tablespoons cornflour
   (cornstarch)**
1 teaspoon salt
**¼ teaspoon five spice
   powder**
1 cup (8 fl oz) oil
**2 spring onions
   (scallions), coarsely
   chopped**
**2 teaspoons finely
   chopped fresh ginger**
Sauce:
2 tablespoons dry sherry
**2 tablespoons light soy
   sauce**
2 teaspoons sugar
2 teaspoons cider vinegar
1 teaspoon sesame oil
Garnish:
**3 tablespoons chopped
   fresh coriander leaves**

Wipe the fish and make deep diagonal cuts on both sides. Combine the cornflour, salt and five spice powder, mixing thoroughly. Sprinkle the trout in this mixture, rubbing it well into the slashes, then dust off the excess.

In a bowl, combine the sauce ingredients; add ½ cup (4 fl oz) water, and stir until the sugar is dissolved.

Heat a wok, add the oil and when hot, slide the fish into the oil and fry on medium heat for 2 minutes until browned on one side; then turn it over and fry the other side for 2 minutes. Remove the fish from the wok.

Pour off all but 1 tablespoon of the oil. When this is very hot, stir-fry the spring onions and ginger for 1 minute; they should not brown. Add the mixed sauce ingredients to the wok and bring to the boil. Return the fish and let it simmer, covered, and on low heat for 5 minutes. Carefully turn the fish over and let it simmer for a further 4 to 5 minutes.

Lift the fish onto a warmed serving dish. The cornflour coating on the fish may have been sufficient to slightly thicken the sauce. If not, mix 1 teaspoon of cornflour with a teaspoon of cold water, stir this into the sauce and allow it to boil up and thicken. Spoon the sauce over the fish, sprinkle liberally with chopped coriander.

Steamed Whole Fish with Mushrooms and Ham

Serves 6–8

1 whole fish, about 2 kg (4 lb) – snapper or red emperor

½ teaspoon salt

1 teaspoon ginger juice

6 dried Chinese mushrooms

1 tablespoon light soy sauce

2 teaspoons sugar

1 teaspoon sesame oil

1 tablespoon Chinese wine or dry sherry

60 g (2 oz) ham

2 spring onions (scallions)

1 tablespoon finely grated fresh ginger

Dipping Sauces:

light soy sauce

grated ginger soaked in 3 tablespoons sherry

sesame oil

chilli oil

Place vegetables and ham into fish scorings.

Place prepared fish on rack.

How to deal with a fish too large to fit into your bamboo steamer.

WASH AND CLEAN THE FISH, wipe with paper towels. Score the fish six times on one side, cutting diagonally into the flesh down to the bone. Rub the fish inside and out with salt and ginger juice, rubbing into the scorings. Set aside.

Soak the mushrooms in hot water for 30 minutes. Drain, but reserve 4 tablespoons of the water; discard the mushroom stems and slice the caps thinly. Put the mushrooms in a small pan; add the soy sauce, sugar and the 4 tablespoons of mushroom soaking water. Bring to the boil, then cover the pan and simmer for 10 minutes. Lift out the mushrooms and set them aside. Add the sesame oil and wine to the liquid left in the pan.

Cut the ham and spring onions into strips. Lightly oil a heatproof dish and place half the ginger, ham and spring onions on the dish. Place the fish on these, uncut side down. Place the mushrooms and the remaining ginger, ham and spring onions in the scorings of fish. Pour the liquid in the pan over the top.

Set a wire rack in a large baking dish and pour in boiling water to a depth of 1.3 cm (½ inch). Place the dish containing the fish on the rack, cover all with a large sheet of aluminium foil, folding the foil over the rim of the baking dish. Place the baking dish on top of the stove and have the heat medium-high so that there is a lot of steam. Cook the fish for about 20 minutes. Remove foil.

Serve with small bowls for the dipping sauces, so that each diner can make his or her own mixture. If liked, garnish with sprigs of fresh coriander or spring onion curls.

Chilli Shrimp and Bamboo Shoot

This highly seasoned mixture, which flavours the bland bean starch (transparent) noodles, is typical of the hot inland provinces of China.

SOAK THE DRIED SHRIMPS in hot water for 30 minutes. Drain well and pat dry with paper towels; pulverise in an electric blender and set aside. Chop the bamboo shoot and set aside.

Separate approximately 60 g (2 oz) bean starch noodles using kitchen shears, place in a pan of boiling water and boil for 15 minutes. Drain and set aside.

Heat a wok, add the peanut oil and swirl to coat the sides of the wok. When hot add the garlic, ginger, powdered shrimp and bamboo shoot; stir-fry for 1 minute. Then add sauce ingredients mixed together, stirring until it boils and thickens. Add sesame oil, stir, and garnish with chopped spring onions.

Place the drained bean starch noodles on a serving dish, and spoon the shrimp mixture over them. Serve immediately.

Serves 4
4 tablespoons dried shrimps
60 g (2 oz) bean starch noodles
250 g (8 oz) canned winter bamboo shoot
2 tablespoons peanut oil
½ teaspoon finely chopped garlic
½ teaspoon finely chopped fresh ginger
few drops of sesame oil
2 tablespoons chopped spring onions (scallions)
Sauce:
2 teaspoons dark soy sauce
½ teaspoon salt
1 teaspoon sugar
½ cup (4 fl oz) chicken stock
2 teaspoons chilli oil
1 teaspoon cornflour (cornstarch)

Chop the bamboo shoot.

Drain boiled bean starch noodles.

Add sauce to the stir-fried mixture.

Layered Seafood with Oyster Sauce

Remove the skin and any small bones from the fish fillets. Slit the prawns along the curve of the back and remove the sandy vein. Finely chop the prawns and put into a bowl with the ginger, chopped spring onions, water chestnuts, salt, cornflour and sesame oil. Mix together thoroughly.

Spread the mixture on the fillets of fish with a spatula or table knife, then use a chopper to cut the fish into pieces of convenient size.

Divide the broccoli into flowerets and slice the broccoli stems thinly. Cut the spring onions into 2.5 cm (1 inch) lengths. Mix together all the sauce ingredients except the cornflour.

Heat about 3 cups (24 fl oz) peanut oil in a wok and when hot, add the pieces of fish (not too many at a time), prawn side downwards. Fry until golden. Remove to paper towels to drain, then arrange on a serving dish and keep warm.

When all the fish has been fried, pour off the oil, leaving about 1 tablespoon. Reheat the oil, add the spring onions and crushed garlic, and stir-fry for 10 seconds. Add the broccoli and fry for a few seconds longer. Then pour in the sauce mixture, bring to the boil, cover the wok and cook for 2 minutes.

Mix the 3 teaspoons of cornflour with 1 tablespoon of cold water, stir this into the sauce until it boils and thickens. Remove from heat. Arrange the broccoli around the fish, then spoon the sauce over, and serve.

Serves 6

500 g (1 lb) fish fillets
250 g (8 oz) shelled raw
  prawns
½ teaspoon finely grated
  fresh ginger
3 tablespoons finely
  chopped spring onion
  (scallion)
2 tablespoons finely
  chopped water
  chestnuts
1 teaspoon salt
1 teaspoon cornflour
  (cornstarch)
1 teaspoon sesame oil
1 bunch broccoli
additional 2 spring onions
  (scallions)
peanut oil for deep frying
½ teaspoon crushed garlic
Sauce:
1 tablespoon oyster sauce
1 cup (8 fl oz) chicken
  stock
1 tablespoon Chinese wine
  or dry sherry
1 teaspoon white vinegar
½ teaspoon sugar
3 teaspoons cornflour
  (cornstarch)

Spread prawn mixture on fish fillets.

Fry fish pieces until golden.

Stir-fry broccoli with spring onion and garlic.

Prawn and Bean Curd Puffs in Oyster Sauce

Drain liquid from bean curd.

Stir bean curd into prawn mixture.

Deep fry mixture until golden.

Serves 4
250 g (8 oz) raw prawns
¼ teaspoon salt
3 teaspoons cornflour (cornstarch)
1 egg
½ teaspoon grated fresh ginger
½ teaspoon sesame oil
250 g (8 oz) fresh bean curd
oil for deep frying
Sauce:
¾ cup (6 fl oz) chicken stock or water
1 tablespoon oyster sauce
1 spring onion (scallion), chopped
1 tablespoon chopped fresh coriander
2 teaspoons cornflour (cornstarch)

Shell and de-vein the prawns. Put them into a food processor with salt, cornflour, egg, ginger and sesame oil; process until all ingredients are minced and the mixture is smooth. Alternatively, the prawns can be chopped very finely and combined with the other ingredients.

Drain the liquid from bean curd and pat dry with paper towels. Add the prawn mixture and stir well together with a fork to mix.

Combine the sauce ingredients except cornflour in a small saucepan, and heat to boiling. Blend the cornflour with 1 tablespoon of cold water and stir it into the sauce until it boils and thickens.

Heat a wok, add enough oil for deep frying and fry spoonfuls of the prawn mixture until they are puffy and golden brown all over. This will have to be done in four or five batches. Drain them well, place on a serving dish and pour the hot sauce over. Serve immediately.

Shrimp with Asparagus and Cloud Ears

Serves 4
500 g (1 lb) shrimps (or small raw prawns)
1 teaspoon crushed garlic
1 teaspoon finely grated fresh ginger
2 tablespoons dried wood fungus
1 bundle tender asparagus
1 medium-sized onion
4 tablespoons peanut oil
Sauce:
2 tablespoons light soy sauce
2 tablespoons Chinese wine or dry sherry
2 tablespoons Oriental sweet chilli sauce
2 teaspoons sesame oil
1 teaspoon cornflour (cornstarch)

Cloud ears, or wood fungus, is a texture ingredient. Having no flavour of its own, it needs to be combined with a robust sauce.

SHELL THE SHRIMPS and de-vein them if necessary. Rinse in cold water and dry on paper towels. Rub the garlic and ginger over the shrimps and set aside.

Soak the wood fungus in water for 10 minutes. Rinse well and trim away any gritty portions. Leave soaking in fresh cold water until required (but drain before use).

Wash the asparagus thoroughly and trim off any tough ends. If necessary, peel the bottom half of each stalk. Cut into bite-size pieces, keeping the tips whole. Peel the onion, cut in half lengthways, then cut each half into six wedge-shaped sections. Mix the sauce ingredients.

Heat a wok and when very hot, add 2 tablespoons of the peanut oil and heat again, swirling to coat the wok. Add the shrimps and stir-fry until they turn pink; then remove from wok.

Add another tablespoon of peanut oil, and stir-fry the drained wood fungus and the onion for 1 minute; remove from wok.

Heat the remaining tablespoon of oil and stir-fry the asparagus on high heat for 1 minute; then turn the heat low, add 3 tablespoons of water and cook, covered, for 3 minutes or until the asparagus is tender but still crisp. If the asparagus is mature it may need a little extra liquid and cooking time, but don't let it become limp.

Return the shrimps to the wok, pour in the sauce ingredients and stir until the sauce boils and thickens slightly. Add the wood fungus and onion, toss through quickly, then serve at once with rice or soft fried noodles.

Unless asparagus is very young, peel with vegetable peeler.

Cut onion half into six wedge-shaped sections.

Stir-fry the asparagus in oil for 1 minute.

Steamed Scallops in Shells

Serves 4–6
250 g (8 oz) scallops
¼ teaspoon grated fresh
   ginger
1 teaspoon oyster sauce
1 tablespoon Chinese wine
   or dry sherry
½ teaspoon sugar
1 spring onion (scallion)
30 g (1 oz) ham

Scallop shells are available very cheaply in kitchenware shops – maybe even on your local beach.

CHECK THE NUMBER of scallops when buying – there should be at least 12, so that each person can have two or more scallops. Remove the dark vein from the scallops but leave the red roe attached.

Combine the ginger, oyster sauce, wine and sugar; add the scallops and stir to mix. Cover and chill for 30 minutes or longer.

Put one or two scallops on each shell (depending on size of the shells) and place them in a bamboo steamer. Cut the spring onion and ham into fine shreds and sprinkle them over the scallops.

Have a wok of boiling water ready, and place the bamboo steamer on this. Cover the steamer and cook over a moderately high heat for 5 minutes. Serve immediately.

Sprinkle scallops with spring onion and ham.

Steam over boiling water.

Crystal Prawns with Snow Peas

Serves 4
500 g (1 lb) raw prawns
salt
1 egg white
1 tablespoon cornflour
   (cornstarch)
1 tablespoon oil
125 g (4 oz) snow peas
1 small clove garlic
pinch of sugar
1 teaspoon finely grated

fresh ginger
oil for deep frying
Sauce:
½ cup (4 fl oz) chicken
   stock
1 tablespoon oyster sauce
1 tablespoon Chinese wine
   or dry sherry
1 teaspoon sesame oil
2 teaspoons cornflour
   (cornstarch)

Like many Chinese recipes, there are two steps and two methods of cooking combined which makes this an ideal dish for preparing ahead, leaving only the final stir-frying to be done at serving time.

SHELL AND DE-VEIN the prawns. Slit them more than halfway through from the outer curve. Put the prawns in a large bowl, sprinkle with 1 teaspoon of salt and stir the prawns briskly for 1 minute.

Transfer prawns to a colander and rinse under cold running water for 1 minute, turning them over and over. Drain, return them to the bowl and sprinkle with another teaspoon of salt. Repeat the procedure, stirring vigorously for 1 minute, then rinse as before. Drain and repeat a third time. (This removes the slippery feel and strong smell that prawns sometimes have.) Dry the prawns.

Now marinate the prawns in a 'velveting' mixture which gives them a protective coating and keeps them moist. Sprinkle them with ½ teaspoon salt. Beat the egg white only enough to break it up, and pour it over the prawns. Sprinkle with the cornflour and mix well. Pour the tablespoon of oil over and mix. Refrigerate for 1 hour.

String the snow peas, wash and dry them. Crush the garlic with sugar. Mix all sauce ingredients together.

Place a wok over high heat until it is very hot. Pour in 3–4 cups (24–32 fl oz) oil and turn the heat to medium. The oil should not be too hot. Drop in the prawns and stir to keep them separate. They will turn white in less than a minute. Lift them immediately from the oil.

Pour off the oil. Wipe out the wok with paper towels and once more place it over high heat. When very hot, add 1 tablespoon of oil and swirl to coat the surface. Add the garlic and ginger, and stir for 10 seconds; then add the snow peas and stir-fry over high heat until they turn a brilliant green (about 1 minute).

Stir the sauce mixture to ensure that the cornflour is smoothly mixed. Pour it into the wok and stir constantly until it boils and thickens. Return the prawns, mix with the sauce and serve immediately with rice.

Sprinkle prawns with salt and stir briskly with chopsticks for 1 minute.

Pour slightly mixed egg white over prawns before adding cornflour.

Fireworks Prawns

A nice touch of fire adds to this particularly tasty seafood dish.

SHELL THE PRAWNS but leaving the tails and last segment of shell. Make a shallow slit and remove the dark vein. Split the prawns halfway through the curve of the back and open them out flat, pressing with the palm of your hand. Cut the rind off the bacon and divide the rashers into pieces about the same size as the prawns. Place a piece of bacon on each prawn, pressing together.

Prepare the batter. Beat the eggs until frothy. Sift the flour and salt together, and add all at once to the eggs, beating until the batter is smooth.

Have the onion and other vegetable ingredients for the sauce ready for stir-frying. Mix together the remaining ingredients for the sauce, stirring honey to dissolve.

Heat a wok, add 2 tablespoons of peanut oil and swirl to coat the sides of the wok. Add the onion, garlic, ginger and chillies and fry over medium low heat, stirring frequently, until the onion pieces are soft and golden. Add the spring onions and fry for 1 minute. Then add the liquid sauce ingredients, allow to boil, stir and remove the sauce from the wok.

Wash the wok, return it to the heat and add 2–3 cups (16–24 fl oz) peanut oil for deep frying. When the oil is hot, dip each prawn together with its bacon into the batter, then drop immediately into the hot oil and deep fry until puffed and golden. Fry a few at a time and remove them as soon as they are done – do not overcook. Drain on absorbent paper.

For convenience, the prawns may be fried and the sauce made an hour or so ahead. Just before serving, reheat the oil until very hot and double-fry the prawns, a few at a time, for just a few seconds. This enhances the crispness. Have sauce ready, reheated in a small pan.

Arrange the prawns on a serving plate and spoon the sauce over. Garnish with spring onion curls.

Press a piece of bacon onto each flattened prawn.

Coat the prawns in batter then deep fry.

Serves 4
500 g (1 lb) large raw
  prawns
6 rashers streaky bacon
peanut oil for cooking
Batter:
2 eggs
½ cup (2 oz) flour
½ teaspoon salt
Sauce:
1 onion, finely chopped
2 teaspoons finely grated
  garlic
2 teaspoons finely grated
  fresh ginger
3 fresh red chillies, seeded
  and sliced

8 spring onions
  (scallions), cut into
  5 cm (2 inch) lengths
½ cup (4 fl oz) tomato
  sauce (ketchup)
2 tablespoons
  Oriental-style sweet
  chilli sauce
2 tablespoons Chinese
  wine or dry sherry
1 tablespoon light soy
  sauce
1 tablespoon honey
¼ teaspoon salt

Lobster in Black Bean Sauce

Serves 4

1 fresh live lobster or frozen raw lobster tail
1 large clove garlic, unpeeled
2 spring onions (scallions)
1 egg
3 slices fresh ginger
4 tablespoons peanut oil
Sauce:
1 tablespoon canned salted black beans
2 cloves garlic
1 teaspoon sugar
1 teaspoon finely grated fresh ginger
¾ cup (6 fl oz) hot stock or water
2 tablespoons Chinese wine or dry sherry
1 tablespoon light soy sauce
2 teaspoons cornflour (cornstarch)

Prepare the lobster (see page 65) – or thaw the frozen lobster tail. Chop straight through where the head joins the body, if using whole lobster. Cut in half lengthways and discard the stomach (in the head) and the feathery tissue. Chop each half of the tail into four or five pieces.

Split the unpeeled garlic clove in two. Cut the spring onions into diagonal slices. Beat the egg slightly, just until mixed.

Prepare the sauce ingredients. Rinse the black beans in a strainer under cold water for a few seconds, drain well, then mash with a fork or chop finely. Crush the 2 cloves of garlic with sugar. Combine the mashed beans, garlic and grated ginger in a small bowl. Mix together the stock (or water), wine and soy sauce. Mix the cornflour smoothly with 1 tablespoon of cold water.

Heat a wok, add the peanut oil and when the oil is hot, fry the halved clove of garlic and the slices of ginger until they are brown; then scoop them out and discard. Add the pieces of lobster to the flavoured oil and stir-fry until the shells are bright red (2 to 3 minutes). Remove to a plate.

Pour off the oil, leaving about 1 tablespoon. Fry the black bean mixture, stirring, until the garlic is fragrant (about 1 minute). Add the liquid ingredients and the pieces of lobster, bring quickly to the boil, then cover the wok and cook on medium heat for 3 minutes.

Uncover pan, stir the cornflour mixture again and pour it into the sauce. Stir until it boils and thickens. Add the spring onions and beaten egg, and stir so that the egg sets in shreds. Serve at once with steamed rice.

If using frozen lobster tail, cut into large pieces.

Finely chop or mash rinsed black beans.

Stir in beaten egg until it sets in shreds.

Deep Fried Lobster with Ginger

There are two ways to treat this recipe. For a delicate result, use only ginger and spring onions. For a more robust flavour, add chillies and garlic. Choose whichever version suits your palate or your mood.

IMMOBILIZE THE LOBSTER by whichever method you choose (see page 65). Chop straight through where the head joins the body. Cut in half lengthways down both body and head. Discard the stomach (to be found in the head) and the feathery tissue. Chop each half of the tail into four or five pieces. Chop off and discard the pointed tips of the legs. Sprinkle the tablespoon of cornflour over the lobster pieces and mix.

Heat a wok, pour in the peanut oil and allow it to get very hot. Discard any fluid that has seeped out of the lobster and drop the pieces into the boiling oil. Scoop the oil over the lobster as it fries. In about 1 to 2 minutes, the shell should turn bright red and the meat loses its transparent look and turns white. The lobster will not be completely cooked at this stage; it finishes cooking with the flavouring ingredients. (If you cook by electricity or your cooker doesn't deliver much heat, it may be better to fry the lobster in two batches, allowing the oil to get very hot again after the first batch has been removed.)

Pour both lobster and oil into a wire sieve set over a heatproof bowl.

Return the wok to the heat with the oil that clings to the sides. Add the ginger, spring onions, chilli and garlic, and stir-fry on high heat for a few seconds. Put in the lobster pieces, pour in the hot chicken stock, cover the wok and cook on high heat for 2–3 minutes so that the lobster finishes cooking in the steam. Uncover and stir. The liquid should be reduced by half.

Blend the cornflour with 1 tablespoon of cold water and stir it into the wok; keep stirring until the sauce boils and thickens. Turn off the heat, take 1 tablespoon of the oil the lobster was fried in and sprinkle it over the lobster. Toss quickly. This gives a nice gloss. Serve immediately.

Serves 4

1 fresh live lobster, about 1 kg (2 lb)
1 tablespoon cornflour (cornstarch)
4 cups (32 fl oz) peanut oil
1 tablespoon fine shreds of fresh ginger
2–3 spring onions (scallions), cut into 5 cm (2 inch) lengths
1 teaspoon sliced hot chilli
1 teaspoon finely chopped garlic
1 cup (8 fl oz) chicken stock, heated
additional 2 teaspoons cornflour (cornstarch)

Chop the lobster tail into pieces.

Ladle oil over lobster as it fries.

Add blended cornflour and stir until sauce boils and thickens.

Saucy Chilli Crab

Serves 4
2 live crabs
½ cup (4 fl oz) peanut oil
2 teaspoons finely grated
   fresh ginger
1½ teaspoons finely
   chopped garlic
3 fresh red chillies, seeded
   and chopped
3 tablespoons chopped
   fresh coriander for
   garnish
Sauce:
½ cup (4 fl oz) tomato
   sauce (ketchup)
3 tablespoons
   Oriental-style chilli
   sauce
1 tablespoon sugar
1 teaspoon salt

Immobilize the crabs (see page 65). Wash them well, scrubbing away any mossy patches on the shell. Remove the hard top shell or carapace, and reserve these for garnishing. Lift the 'apron' with the tip of a knife and twist off, together with the dark vein. Discard the stomach bag and the feathery grey gills arranged in two rows. Twist off the large claws and chop each claw in half at the joint. Crack the shells with blunt edge of a cleaver so that the sauce can penetrate. Chop the bodies in half down the middle, then cut each half in two again, crossways. Leave legs attached but chop off the pointed tips.

Stir the sauce ingredients together to dissolve the sugar, adding ¼ cup (2 fl oz) hot water.

Heat a wok, add the peanut oil and when the oil is hot, fry each carapace until it turns a bright red, just a few seconds. Lift out and reserve. Add the pieces of crab and stir-fry, turning them to cook on all sides until the shells are bright red and the flesh is white and opaque. Remove to a plate.

Turn the heat to low, add the ginger, garlic and chillies and fry until they are cooked but not brown. Add the sauce mixture. Return the crab pieces and spoon the sauce over them until all are coated. Cover the wok and cook on low heat for 2 to 3 minutes. Arrange on a serving dish and garnish with top shell. Sprinkle with chopped coriander leaves, and serve with steamed rice.

To remove top shell, insert knife at back seam and twist.

Crack the claws with cleaver.

Cut each crab half into two, crossways.

Stir-Fried Prawns with Broccoli and Red Ginger

Serves 4
12–16 large raw prawns
1 head firm, fresh broccoli
1 tablespoon peanut oil
½ teaspoon finely grated fresh ginger
1 tablespoon fine strips of red ginger
Sauce:
¼ cup (2 fl oz) water
2 tablespoons Chinese wine or dry sherry
1 tablespoons light soy sauce
1 tablespoon oyster sauce
½ teaspoon sugar
2 teaspoons cornflour (cornstarch) or arrowroot
1 tablespoon cold water

Shell and de-vein the prawns, leaving the tails on. With the point of a sharp knife make a small slit through the underside of the prawns.

Wash the broccoli and shake dry. Divide into flowerets, leaving a piece of tender green stalk on each. Pass the end of the stem through the slit in the prawn so that the floweret rests within the curve.

Heat the wok and add the oil. When the oil is hot, add the ginger and stir, then immediately add the prawns threaded with broccoli. Stir-fry for 2 minutes. Add all the sauce ingredients mixed together, except the cornflour and cold water. Turn the heat to medium low, cover and simmer for 3 minutes. Push the prawns to the side of the wok, add the cornflour mixed smoothly with cold water and stir until thick. Serve at once, garnished with red ginger and accompanied by white rice.

Shell and de-vein the prawns, leaving the tails on.

Using a sharp knife, make a small slit through the underside of the prawns.

Pass a broccoli floweret through each prawn.

Chilli Squid

Serves 4
500 g (1 lb) medium-sized
  squid
½ teaspoon salt
1 egg white
1½ tablespoons cornflour
  (cornstarch)
1½ tablespoons peanut oil
1 small red capsicum
  (sweet pepper)
1 clove garlic
6 spring onions (scallions)
1 tablespoon bottled
  preserved hot radish
12 snow peas (mange-tout)
  or tender green beans
2 fresh red chillies for
  garnish
Sauce:
½ cup (4 fl oz) light stock
  or water
½ teaspoon each salt and
  sugar
1 teaspoon chilli oil or 1
  tablespoon chilli sauce
2 teaspoons cornflour
  (cornstarch) or
  arrowroot

Hold down the head of the squid with the blunt edge of a knife and pull the body. The head and contents of sac will come away. Reserve the tentacles and discard everything else. Slit the body of the squid lengthways and rinse well.

On the inside surface make diagonal cuts with a sharp knife held at a 45° angle, parallel to each other and about 6 mm (¼ inch) apart. Then score across these lines to make a pattern of small diamonds or squares. Take care not to cut through the squid. After scoring, divide the squid into neat pieces, about 5 cm × 2.5 cm (2 inch × 1 inch).

In a bowl, mix the squid with salt, egg white, cornflour and peanut oil. Refrigerate for at least 30 minutes.

Cut the capsicum into thin strips and the spring onions into bite-size lengths. String the snow peas. Crush the garlic with a little salt.

Heat a wok over high heat, pour in about 3 cups peanut oil and when the oil is moderately hot, drop in the squid, stirring to separate the pieces. In less than a minute they will curl and the scoring forms an attractive pattern. It is important not to overcook or the squid will toughen. Drain on a wire spoon placed over a heatproof bowl.

Return the wok to the heat with just the oil that clings to the sides. Stir-fry the garlic, capsicum, spring onions and snow peas for 1 minute, add the preserved hot radish and stir. Add the sauce ingredients mixed together and stir constantly until it boils and thickens. Return the squid to the pan and mix with the sauce.

Arrange on a serving dish, garnish with chilli flowers and serve immediately with plain steamed rice.

Note: As an indication of the fiery nature of a dish, I like to garnish it with chilli flowers but remember to slit and soak chillies in ice water some hours before required, as they take time to curl.

Hold the squid head and pull the body with the other hand. The head and contents of the sac will come away.

Score the body of the squid in a diamond pattern.

The squid will curl when cooked in hot oil. Do not overcook.

Stir-fry garlic, capsicum, spring onions, snow peas.

Poultry

Chicken, duck, pigeon, all are prized in Chinese cuisine. One of the most imaginative ways of cooking duck is the famous Peking Duck. It requires specially bred ducks, special barrel-shaped ovens, and the chef's ability to blow air between the skin and the flesh of the bird to make authentic Peking Duck. The most the home cook can do is an approximate recipe, but there is nothing against serving any style of roast duck in the manner of Peking Duck. The crisp skin with its underlayer of melting fat is cut into small pieces and wrapped in Mandarin Pancakes which are brushed with hoi sin sauce. Shreds of crisp cucumber and spring onions (scallions) are also enclosed in the wrapping. The combination is delicious.

The flesh of the duck is served in a stir-fried dish, and the carcase used to make a soup. Thus one duck provides three courses.

In western cooking a chicken is roasted or stewed from stem to stern. In Chinese cooking, different parts of the bird are chosen for different treatment. Sensible, since wings and legs and thighs need longer cooking than delicate breast meat.

Most supermarkets sell the separate joints, but for those to whom this service is not available, the answer is to joint two or three chickens and use the various part separately, freezing what cannot be used immediately until it is needed. It is worth the extra effort.

Chicken cooked Chinese style is a revelation of how to put back flavour into what used to be a special-occasion bird but which, with mass production and raising methods far removed from the free-range style, have resulted in a rather bland product.

Left: clockwise from front: olive nuts; Szechwan peppercorns; dried tangerine peel; dried chillies; Peking Duck with Mandarin Pancakes (see page 141), plum sauce and spring onion brushes; fresh chillies; Crisp Skin Chicken (see page 95); shredded chicken and vegetables in wok; Chinese cabbage; red pepper (capsicum).

Chicken Livers with Bamboo Shoot and Cabbage

Serves 4

500 g (1 lb) chicken livers
2 slices fresh ginger
1 spring onion (scallion)
3 tablespoons dark soy
** sauce**
1 canned winter bamboo
** shoot**
1 bunch gai choy (mustard
** cabbage)**
1 tablespoon sugar
1 tablespoon Chinese wine
** or dry sherry**
2 tablespoons peanut oil
1 teaspoon cornflour
** (cornstarch)**
2 teaspoons sesame oil
1 tablespoon white vinegar

Halve the chicken livers and remove any tubes, connective tissue and yellow spots. Put the livers into a small saucepan with the ginger, spring onion cut into three or four pieces, and 1 tablespoon of the soy sauce. Add enough boiling water to just cover the livers. Simmer, covered, over a low heat for 5 minutes. Drain and discard ginger and onion.

Slice the bamboo shoot. Wash the gai choy and slice diagonally; there should be about 3 cups. Combine the remaining 2 tablespoons of soy sauce, sugar and wine.

Heat a wok, add the peanut oil and swirl it around the sides of the wok. Toss in the chicken livers and stir-fry for 10 seconds. Add the soy mixture, bamboo shoot and gai choy, and stir-fry for 2 minutes. Blend the cornflour with 2 teaspoons of cold water and add this to the livers, stirring until the sauce thickens. Add sesame oil.

Sprinkle the vinegar around the edge of the wok and, as it sizzles, give the livers a few fast turns. Turn out into a dish to serve.

Halve the chicken livers.

Cut gai choy into slices.

Chicken Velvet Fu Yung

Serves 4

1 large chicken breast, about 375 g (12 oz)
1 teaspoon salt
2 teaspoons water chestnut flour or cornflour (cornstarch)
1 tablespoon Chinese wine or dry sherry
4 eggs, separated
1 stem celery
1 Chinese cabbage or lettuce
peanut oil for cooking
1 teaspoon sugar
½ teaspoon salt
Sauce:
stock made with chicken skin and bones
1 teaspoon light soy sauce
3 teaspoons cornflour (cornstarch)

Scrape chicken flesh finely.

Stir whipped egg whites into chicken mixture.

Chop cooked egg yolk with wok chan.

'Chicken velvet' is a term that describes very finely puréed chicken meat which has been lightened by the addition of water and egg whites. When cooked, it is similar to a soft custard. ('Velveting', on the other hand, is a method of marinating and coating.) Fu Yung is a white hibiscus and this dish is so named because the chicken should remain white when cooked.

REMOVE THE SKIN and bones from the chicken breast. When boning, hold a sharp knife close to the bone.

Take the small fillet from each side of the breast and, holding the silvery tendon, scrape the flesh finely. Discard tendon.

Place the large fillets on the chopping board, with the side that was next to the skin downwards. Again use the sharp chopper to scrape the flesh free of the long fibres that lie against the skin.

Put the skin, bones and discarded fibres into a small pan with about 1½ cups (12 fl oz) cold water to cover, and simmer to give the 1 cup (8 fl oz) chicken stock needed for the sauce. Strain and season to taste with salt.

Finely chop the chicken meat, first one way and then the other, until it is a fine purée. Gradually add 1 tablespoon of cold water while chopping, to lighten the consistency. Add the salt and wine. Add the water chestnut flour or cornflour mixed smoothly with 1 tablespoon of cold water, stirring to mix.

In a large bowl whip the whites of the eggs until frothy and holding soft peaks. Stir a large spoonful at a time into the chicken mixture until all the egg white is incorporated. Cover and chill for 30 minutes or longer.

Beat the yolks with a little salt and set aside. Cut the celery into thin slices. Cut the cabbage or lettuce into chunky pieces.

Heat a wok, add 1 tablespoon of peanut oil and stir the egg yolk over medium heat until it sets. Do not brown. Remove from heat, cut into small pieces with the sharp edge of a wok chan.

Heat another tablespoon of peanut oil and stir-fry the celery for 1 minute, not allowing it to brown; set aside.

Heat 2 more tablespoons of peanut oil and stir-fry the cabbage or lettuce for 1 minute. Sprinkle with the·sugar and salt. Add 2 tablespoons of water, cover the wok and leave for 30 seconds for lettuce or 2 to 3 minutes for a firmer green vegetable. Spread on the serving dish.

Clean out the wok, return it to the heat and when hot, pour in ½ cup (4 fl oz) peanut oil. Do not let the oil become too hot – the aim is to keep the chicken from browning. Pour in the chicken velvet and turn it quickly with the wok chan until it is white. Pour it through a wire strainer and let all excess oil drain out.

Meanwhile combine the sauce ingredients including 1 cup of chicken stock, and bring to a boil in a small saucepan, stirring until thick and clear. Toss the chicken velvet with celery and yolk pieces, spread over the green vegetable, and pour the sauce over. Serve at once with rice.

Braised Ginger Chicken

Cut the chicken into bite-size pieces. Scrape the skin off the ginger and cut the ginger into thin slices, then into fine shreds until you have about ¼ cup. Set aside. Crush the garlic with a sprinkling of salt.

Heat the peppercorns lightly in a dry pan. Then crush them with a pestle and mortar or on a wooden chopping board using the handle of a heavy chopper.

Heat a wok over high heat, add the peanut oil and fry the shredded ginger and crushed garlic over low heat until pale golden. Add the chicken pieces, raise the heat to medium and fry until the chicken changes colour. Add pepper, wine, honey, soy sauce and star anise. Cover the wok and simmer over low heat for 25 minutes or until the chicken is tender, adding a little hot water toward end of cooking if necessary. Serve with hot steamed rice.

Serves 6

1 × 1.5 kg (3 lb) roasting chicken
1 piece fresh tender ginger
1 clove garlic
½ teaspoon Szechwan peppercorns or black peppercorns
3 tablespoons peanut oil
¼ cup (2 fl oz) Chinese wine or dry sherry
1 tablespoon honey
¼ cup (2 fl oz) light soy sauce
1 star anise

Cut ginger into fine shreds.

Fry chicken until it changes colour.

Chicken with Peppery Turnips

Finely chop the peppery turnips.

Separate the soaked noodles so they cook evenly.

Serves 4
500 g (1 lb) chicken breast or thighs
½ teaspoon salt
1 tablespoon egg white
2 teaspoons cornflour (cornstarch)
peanut oil for mixing and cooking – about ½ cup (4 fl oz)
12 green beans
1 small carrot
2 tablespoons sesame seeds
2 teaspoons finely grated fresh ginger
2 tablespoons peppery turnips
3 small bundles fine egg noodles, about 185 g (6 oz)
2 spring onions (scallions), coarsely chopped
Sauce:
stock made with chicken skin and bones
1 tablespoon light soy sauce
1 tablespoon Chinese wine or dry sherry
2 teaspoons oyster sauce
2 teaspoons cornflour (cornstarch)

If you like your dishes with a dash of fire, introduce peppery turnips or preserved hot radish or preserved Szechwan vegetable. They come in jars or cans and all add an interesting flavour.

SKIN AND BONE the chicken pieces and cut the chicken meat into small dice. Place in a bowl and mix in the salt and egg white. Then add the cornflour and mix again. Add 2 teaspoons of peanut oil and mix. Cover the bowl and chill for at least 30 minutes.

Make a small quantity of stock from the chicken skin and bones and about 1 cup (8 fl oz) water.

Top and tail the beans and string them if necessary; cut them into small slices. Dice the carrot to make pieces of similar size. Cook the beans and the carrots separately in a little boiling water for 1 or 2 minutes, just until half-tender. Drain, and place them in ice-cold water to set their colour.

Toast the sesame seeds in a dry pan over low heat until golden. Remove from the pan and set aside.

Soak the grated ginger in 1 tablespoon of cold water, then squeeze out the juice through a small strainer. Finely chop the peppery turnips.

Soak the noodles in hot water to loosen and separate the strands. Bring a saucepan of water to the boil with a little salt and 1 teaspoon of peanut oil. Drain the noodles and drop them into the boiling water, boil for 2 minutes or until just cooked, not mushy. Run cold water over to cool, drain well.

Heat a wok, add 2 tablespoons of peanut oil and swirl to coat the sides of the wok. When the oil is hot, add the noodles, tossing and stirring to heat them through. Place on a serving dish, cover with foil and keep warm.

Mix the sauce ingredients together, including ½ cup (4 fl oz) chicken stock.

Heat the wok again, add 3 tablespoons of peanut oil. When the oil is moderately hot, add the chicken meat and stir for 1 minute or just until it has turned white. Add the green beans, carrots, ginger juice and turnips and stir-fry for 30 seconds. Add the sauce mixture and the spring onions, stirring while the sauce boils and thickens. Ladle it over the noodles. Sprinkle with the toasted sesame seeds and serve at once.

Home-Style Steamed Chicken

Serves 4 as part of a Chinese meal, serves 2 as a single dish with rice

half a 1.5 kg (3 lb) roasting chicken

2 teaspoons light soy sauce

2 teaspoons Chinese wine or dry sherry

2 teaspoons cornflour (cornstarch)

1 teaspoon finely chopped fresh ginger

½ teaspoon salt

½ teaspoon sugar

½ teaspoon sesame oil, optional

A quick and easy dish with hardly any preparation – delicately flavoured and popular with children as well as grown-ups.

PLACE THE HALF-CHICKEN on a wooden chopping board and separate the thigh and drumstick from the body. Detach the wing, too. With a sharp, heavy cleaver, chop straight through the bones, cutting the chicken into bite-size pieces. Wipe all cut surfaces with damp paper towels to remove any bits of bone.

Put the chicken on a plate, add all the other ingredients and mix well.

Place the plate in a bamboo or other steamer, or on a trivet or upturned bowl in a large pan containing boiling water. Cover the pan with a lid and steam on high heat for 15 minutes.

If liked, place some Chinese vegetables or chunks of peeled pumpkin on the plate with the chicken. Serve hot with steamed rice.

Chop chicken into small pieces.

Steam the chicken over boiling water.

Red Cooked Chicken and Mushrooms

Serves 4–6
8–10 large dried Chinese mushrooms
1 × 1.5 kg (3 lb) chicken
1½ cups (12 fl oz) dark soy sauce
⅓ cup Chinese wine or dry sherry
2 teaspoons sesame oil
5 cm (2 inch) piece fresh ginger, peeled and sliced
1 clove garlic, peeled
1 whole star anise
2 tablespoons sugar
additional 2 teaspoons sesame oil
1 tablespoon peanut oil
Chinese cabbage

Baste chicken frequently with the cooking liquid.

Cut cooked chicken into bite-size pieces.

Cut cabbage into sections.

Red cooking is done in quite a large amount of soy sauce, but it must be dark soy or the dish would not have its rich colour and the proper flavour. Light soy sauce is more salty, too. While it may seem like an extravagant use of soy sauce, the cooking liquid that remains is a Master Sauce. It can be frozen and used over and over again to simmer meats and poultry.

SOAK THE MUSHROOMS in 1½ cups (12 fl oz) boiling water for 30 minutes. Drain and reserve the liquid.

Wash the chicken under cold running water and drain well. Cut off the mushroom stems and put them into the cavity of the chicken for flavouring. These will be discarded after cooking.

Choose a saucepan into which the chicken will just fit so that the liquid will cover as much of the bird as possible. Put the chicken into the saucepan breast down, then add the liquid from the mushrooms, the soy sauce, wine, 2 teaspoons of sesame oil, ginger, garlic, star anise, sugar and the mushroom caps. Bring slowly to the boil, then turn the heat low, cover the saucepan and simmer very gently for 15 minutes.

Using tongs, turn the chicken over, replace the lid and simmer for 20 minutes more. Baste the breast of the chicken with liquid every 5 minutes.

Remove from the heat and leave covered in the saucepan until cool. Lift the chicken on to a chopping board and cut it in half lengthways. Discard the mushroom stems. Brush over the chicken with the remaining 2 teaspoons of sesame oil, then cut each half into bite-size pieces through the bones, using a cleaver.

Bring a large saucepan of lightly salted water to the boil, add the peanut oil. Boil 6–8 leaves of cabbage for 2 minutes uncovered. The colour of the leaves will be bright and the texture still crisp. Drain, and place them on chopping board in a neat pile. Cut across into bite-size sections.

Arrange the cabbage around the edge of a serving plate. Remove the mushroom caps from the sauce with a slotted spoon and place on top. Arrange the chicken pieces in the centre of the plate. Some of the Master Sauce may be served in small bowls as a dipping sauce.

Braised Chicken with Five Flavours

Serves 6
1 × 1.3 kg (2½ lb) chicken
1 mandarin or orange
1 teaspoon Szechwan
   peppercorns
2 tablespoons oil
3 teaspoons finely
   chopped fresh ginger
3 dried red chillies
3 fresh red chillies
3 spring onions
   (scallions), finely sliced
1 teaspoon salt
Sauce:
2 tablespoons Chinese
   wine or dry sherry
2 tablespoons dark soy
   sauce
1 teaspoon sugar
juice from the mandarin
   or orange
2 teaspoons sesame oil

Not all Chinese food must be made and served at once. Here is a good do-ahead dish.

CUT THE CHICKEN in half lengthways, then chop through the bones into pieces about 2.5 cm (1 inch) wide.

Squeeze 2 tablespoons of juice from the mandarin and set this aside for the sauce. Finely shred the orange portion of the rind, first removing all the white pith.

Roast the peppercorns in a dry pan until fragrant. Pound them with a pestle and mortar or with the handle of a cleaver.

Heat a wok, add the peanut oil and swirl to coat the sides of the wok. When the oil is hot, put in the ginger, dried and fresh chillies, shredded rind and half of the spring onions. Toss for about 10 seconds. Add half the chicken pieces, brown over high heat and remove from the wok.

Brown the remaining chicken pieces, then return the first batch of chicken to the wok and sprinkle with salt and the Szechwan pepper. Mix together the ingredients for the sauce, except sesame oil, and pour in. Cover the wok and simmer for 25 to 30 minutes, turning the pieces of chicken every 10 minutes so that they will be evenly coloured. Add remaining spring onions.

Uncover and, if sauce is thin, cook on high heat for a few minutes, stirring, until it becomes thick and syrupy. Turn off the heat, remove and discard the chillies, add sesame oil and mix well. Serve with hot steamed rice.

If not serving the dish straight away, remove from the wok and reheat before serving.

Finely shred the mandarin rind.

Pound roasted peppercorns with the handle of a cleaver.

Sprinkle salt and ground peppercorns over chicken.

Lemon Chicken with Olive Nuts

Bone the chicken and remove the skin. Cut the chicken into finger-width strips. Place the pieces in a bowl, add the salt, ginger and egg yolks; mix well. Sprinkle the cornflour over and mix again. Cover the bowl and chill for at least 30 minutes.

Combine sauce ingredients in a small bowl, with 9 tablespoons of water.

Heat a wok, add about 2 cups (16 fl oz) peanut oil and when hot, drop in the chicken, one piece at a time until one-third of the pieces have been added. Fry over medium heat until the chicken meat is cooked through but do not allow to brown – cut a piece of chicken in half to test. Drain the cooked pieces, then cook remaining chicken meat in the same way.

When chicken has been removed from the wok, turn the heat very low and fry the olive nuts to a pale golden colour. Lift out on to absorbent paper. Drain the oil into a heatproof container.

Return the wok to the heat, pour in the sauce mixture, first giving it a little stir to ensure that the cornflour is not settled at the bottom. Stir until it boils and thickens. Add the lemon slices and sesame oil. Return the chicken meat and olive nuts, toss quickly to coat, and serve immediately. Garnish with fresh coriander and extra lemon slices.

Serves 4–6
750 g (1½ lb) chicken thighs or 500 g (1 lb) chicken breasts
1 teaspoon salt
½ teaspoon grated fresh ginger
2 egg yolks
2 tablespoons cornflour (cornstarch)
peanut oil for deep frying
30 g (1 oz) Chinese olive nuts or pine nuts
6 lemon slices
1 teaspoon sesame oil
Lemon Sauce:
2 tablespoons lemon juice
1½ tablespoons sugar
2 teaspoons light soy sauce
2 drops yellow food colouring
1 tablespoon cornflour (cornstarch)
Garnish:
sprigs of fresh coriander
additional lemon slices

Cut the chicken into finger-width strips.

Deep fry the chicken pieces until cooked but not brown.

Chinese olive nuts.

Chicken with Pecans

Remove bones from chicken breasts.

Cut each straw mushroom in half.

Remove strings from snow peas.

Serves 4–5

500 g (1 lb) chicken breast
½ teaspoon salt
1 tablespoon Chinese wine
or dry sherry
1 egg white
1 tablespoon cornflour
(cornstarch)
2 cups (16 fl oz) peanut oil
1 cup drained canned
straw mushrooms
125 g (4 oz) snow peas
1 cup (3 oz) pecan halves
1 teaspoon crushed garlic
1 teaspoon grated fresh
ginger
Sauce:
stock made with chicken
skin and bones
1 tablespoon oyster sauce
1 tablespoon Chinese wine
or dry sherry
1 teaspoon cornflour
(cornstarch)

Remove the skin and bones from the chicken and cut the chicken meat into small dice. Place in a bowl and season with the salt and wine. Beat the egg white slightly and add to chicken, mixing well. Leave for 10 minutes.

Mix the cornflour into the chicken. Add 1 tablespoon of the peanut oil and mix, then refrigerate for at least 30 minutes.

Make a small quantity of stock from the chicken skin and bones and about 1 cup (8 fl oz) water.

Drain the straw mushrooms well and cut each in half. Remove the strings from the snow peas.

Heat the remaining peanut oil in a wok and fry the pecans over a medium heat, taking care not to burn them. Remove when golden, and drain.

In the same oil over medium heat, deep fry the chicken, stirring to separate pieces, just until the meat turns white. Drain.

Pour off all but 1 tablespoon of oil. Fry the garlic and ginger in this remaining oil until golden. Add the straw mushrooms and stir-fry for 2 minutes. Add the snow peas and stir-fry for 1 minute.

Combine the ingredients for the sauce including ½ cup (4 fl oz) chicken stock; add this to the wok and stir until the sauce boils and thickens.

Return the chicken to the wok and stir with other ingredients just until heated through. Turn off the heat, toss in the pecans, mix through and serve immediately.

Note: For a more pungent flavour, toss the fried pecans while hot in a mixture of ½ teaspoon garlic salt and ½ teaspoon chilli powder.

Deep Fried Crisp-Skin Chicken

Serves 4–6

1 × 1 kg (2 lb) frying chicken
1 teaspoon salt
2½ teaspoons five spice powder
2 teaspoons ground cinnamon
1 teaspoon cayenne pepper
2 tablespoons honey
1 lemon, sliced
peanut oil for deep frying
Salt and Spice Mix:
2 tablespoons salt
1 teaspoon Szechwan peppercorns
½ teaspoon five spice powder
Garnish:
sprigs of fresh coriander
lemon wedges

Pour hot honey mixture over chicken.

Lower chicken into wok and ladle oil over.

Chop chicken into strips to serve.

Wash the chicken and wipe it with paper towels inside and out. Mix the salt with ½ teaspoon of the five spice powder and rub this inside the chicken. Place it in a large heatproof bowl.

Bring to the boil 6 cups (1.5 litres) water with the cinnamon, cayenne pepper and the remaining 2 teaspoons of five spice powder; and pour it over the chicken. Leave the chicken in this while bringing to the boil 4 more cups (1 litre) water with the honey and lemon slices.

Drain the chicken from the spice mixture and put it in a colander. Slowly pour the honey mixture over, making sure it comes into contact with all parts of the chicken. Put it on a wire rack in an airy place to dry – in front of a window or in the sunlight would be ideal. Leave it to dry for 5 hours.

Tie the legs of the chicken together, leaving sufficient string to hold it with while frying. Shortly before serving, heat about 8 cups of peanut oil in a wok and lower the bird into the oil. With a ladle, spoon oil over the chicken as it cooks, and turn it so that it is cooked and brown on all sides. On medium heat the chicken should be cooked through in about 12 to 15 minutes. Test by piercing with a fine skewer where the thigh joins the body. If the juice runs out clear, the chicken is done; but if it is pink, return the chicken to the pan for further cooking.

Lift on to a board with a slotted spoon and cut the chicken in half lengthways with a heavy chopper. Place each half with cut side downwards on the board and chop through into strips 2.5 cm (1 inch) wide. Reassemble the bird on a serving dish. Garnish with fresh coriander sprigs and serve immediately.

Serve with Salt and Spice Mix (see below) and wedges of lemon. The pieces of chicken are sprinkled with a pinch of the salt mix and a few drops of lemon juice by each diner before eating.

Salt and Spice Mix: Put the peppercorns and salt into a small heavy pan over very low heat and roast, shaking the pan, until very hot and the salt starts to colour slightly. Remove the pan from the heat and allow the mixture to cool. When cold, grind with a pestle and mortar or put into a plastic bag and crush with a rolling pin. Mix in the five spice powder. Store in a jar with well-fitting lid.

Chicken with Bean Sprouts and Mixed Pickles

Bone the chicken thighs and discard the skin – or buy chicken thigh fillets. Freeze the meat until firm.

Slice the chicken meat thinly, place it in a bowl and mix in the ginger, wine, salt and cornflour.

Cut the capsicum into shreds. Remove the tails from the bean sprouts.

Combine all the sauce ingredients in a small bowl, with 2 tablespoons of water.

Heat a wok, add the peanut oil and when hot, fry the chicken mixture, stirring constantly for about 1 minute. Add the capsicum and the pickles. Stir in the bean sprouts. Add the sauce mixture and stir over high heat for 1 minute or until the liquid thickens and becomes clear. Serve immediately.

Serves 4
500 g (1 lb) chicken thighs
1 teaspoon grated ginger
1 tablespoon Chinese wine or dry sherry
½ teaspoon salt
2 teaspoons cornflour (cornstarch)
1 small red capsicum (red pepper)
250 g (8 oz) bean sprouts

2 tablespoons peanut oil
3 tablespoons sliced Chinese mixed pickles
Sauce:
2 tablespoons Chinese wine or dry sherry
1 tablespoon light soy sauce
½ teaspoon sugar
2 teaspoons cornflour (cornstarch)

Chinese mixed pickles.

Slice chicken meat thinly.

Remove tails from bean sprouts.

Hunan-Style Chicken

Serves 4–6

1 kg (2 lb) chicken thighs, boned
1 teaspoon Szechwan peppercorns
½ teaspoon salt
2 tablespoons dark soy sauce
2 tablespoons Chinese wine or dry sherry
2 teaspoons sugar
2 tablespoons peanut oil
1 or 2 dried red chillies

2 tablespoons finely chopped spring onions (scallions)
2 teaspoons finely chopped fresh ginger
1 teaspoon finely chopped garlic
1 teaspoon sesame oil
2 tablespoons Chinese black vinegar or 1 tablespoon wine vinegar
1 small teaspoon chilli bean sauce

Like the food of its better-known neighbour, Szechwan province, the food of this western area is hot and spicy to contend with the hot and humid climate. This dish is not too pungent and well worth trying.

FOR THIS RECIPE, the dark meat is best and it is possible to buy filleted thighs in some poultry shops. If these are not available, buy thighs and drumsticks, allowing about 250 g (8 oz) extra for the bones. Leave the skin on but remove all the bones, keeping the knife close to the bone so that little meat is wasted.

Lay the boned pieces on wooden chopping board, skin side down, and flatten them slightly by pounding with the blunt edge of a cleaver or with a meat mallet. Cut into bite-size pieces.

Roast the peppercorns in a dry pan for a few minutes, shaking the pan, until fragrant. Allow to cool, then grind them with a pestle and mortar. Mix with the salt, and sprinkle this over the chicken pieces. Mix and leave for 5 minutes.

Combine the soy sauce, wine and sugar, stir to dissolve the sugar, and pour over the chicken. Turn the chicken pieces well in the marinade. Leave for 30 minutes.

Heat a wok, add the peanut oil and swirl to coat the sides of the wok. Fry the dried chillies for 1 minute. Add the spring onions, ginger and garlic and stir-fry for 10 seconds. Add the chicken together with the marinade and on high heat, stir-fry for a few minutes, just until all the chicken has come into contact with the hot pan. Turn the heat to low, cover the wok and simmer for about 5 minutes or until the chicken is tender.

Meanwhile, mix together the sesame oil, vinegar and chilli bean sauce.

Uncover the wok and if liquid is not thick, raise the heat and turn the chicken pieces over and over using a wok chan. The sauce will become thick and coat the chicken.

Add the sesame oil combination and mix quickly but thoroughly. Transfer to a serving dish immediately and, if liked, discard the dry chillies. Serve with rice and a dish of vegetables.

Flatten boned chicken with cleaver.

Marinate chicken pieces in soy mixture for 30 minutes.

Duck with Tangerine Sauce

Serves 4–6

1 × 1.75 kg (3¾ lb) duck
½ teaspoon salt
½ teaspoon pepper
1 teaspoon grated fresh
  ginger
2 tablespoons cornflour
  (cornstarch)
oil for deep frying
Sauce:
2 tablespoons light soy
  sauce
1 tablespoon sugar
4 tablespoons Chinese
  wine or dry sherry
juice of 3 mandarins or 2
  oranges
1 piece dried tangerine
  peel
Garnish:
segments of mandarin or
  orange

With a sharp cleaver, chop the duck into 12–14 pieces. Discard the tail. (Neck and wing tips may be added to the stock pot.) Rub the pieces of duck with salt, pepper and ginger, and leave for 2 hours.

Blend 1 teaspoon of the cornflour with 1 tablespoon water and set aside. Toss the duck pieces in the remaining cornflour.

Deep fry four pieces at a time for 3 to 4 minutes. Drain on paper towels.

In a saucepan, combine the sauce ingredients with 1 cup (8 fl oz) water, bring to the boil and simmer for 2 minutes. Add the duck pieces, cover the saucepan and simmer for 30 to 40 minutes or until the duck is tender. Remove the tangerine peel. Stir the reserved cornflour and water, and mix it into the sauce until it boils and thickens. Serve garnished with mandarin or orange segments gently heated in the sauce if liked.

Chop the duck into 12–14 pieces.

Deep fry floured duck pieces.

Duck with Sweet Hot Plum Sauce

Wash the duck well. Cut off and discard the tail. Dry inside and out with paper towels. Combine salt, soy sauce, wine and five spice powder, and rub all over the duck, inside and out. Leave to marinate for at least 1 hour so the flavours can penetrate.

Put the duck on a steamer rack and steam for 1½ to 2 hours or until tender.

Set the duck aside to cool and when cool enough to handle, dry it thoroughly with paper towels. Dredge the duck with cornflour.

Heat oil in a wok and when very hot, gently lower the duck into the oil. Keep ladling hot oil over the top of the duck. Turn it when the underside is done, and fry the other side in the same manner until the skin is crisp. Lift it out of the oil with a slotted spoon, allowing the oil to drain back into the wok.

Chop the duck in half lengthways, then chop each half into bite-size pieces. Arrange on a serving platter and spoon the sauce over.

Sauce: Heat the 1 tablespoon of oil and gently fry the ginger and garlic until fragrant (about 1 minute). Stir in the plum sauce and chilli sauce plus 1 tablespoon of water, until the sauce boils. Simmer for 1 minute. Serve with rice and garnish, if liked, with carrot flowers.

Serves 4–5
1 × 2 kg (4 lb) duck
1½ teaspoons salt
1 tablespoon light soy sauce
2 teaspoons Chinese wine or dry sherry
1 teaspoon five spice powder
2 tablespoons cornflour (cornstarch)
oil for deep frying
spring onions or fresh coriander for garnish
Sauce:
1 tablespoon oil
1 teaspoon finely grated fresh ginger
½ teaspoon crushed garlic
3 tablespoons plum sauce
1 teaspoon Chinese chilli sauce

Rub duck inside and out with spice mixture.

Ladle hot oil over duck until skin is crisp.

Braised Duck with Sweet Potatoes

Red bean curd.

Add the bean curd mixture to the browned duck, then pour in water.

Cut the duck into pieces, Chinese style.

Serves 6

1 × 2 kg (4 lb) duck
2 cloves garlic, crushed
1 teaspoon finely grated
    fresh ginger
1 tablespoon light soy
    sauce
1 tablespoon Chinese wine
    or dry sherry
750 g (1½ lb) sweet
    potatoes
½ cup (4 fl oz) peanut oil
3 tablespoons red bean
    curd
2 teaspoons sugar
vegetable flowers for
    garnishing

If the duck has been frozen, allow it to thaw completely. Rinse the duck and wipe inside and out with paper towels. Combine the garlic, ginger, soy sauce and wine, and rub all over the duck, inside and out.

Peel the sweet potatoes, cut them into 5 cm (2 inch) slices and drop into a bowl of cold water.

Heat the oil in a wok and brown the duck all over, turning it frequently. Remove duck to a dish.

Pour off most of the oil, leaving only a little. Return the duck to the wok. Add the bean curd mashed with the sugar. Pour in hot water to come halfway up the duck. Bring to the boil, then reduce the heat, cover the wok and simmer for 1 hour. Turn the duck during cooking, and add more boiling water if necessary.

Drain the sweet potatoes, add them to the wok, and simmer for a further 15 to 30 minutes or until the duck is tender.

Lift the duck on to a wooden board and cut it into pieces with a sharp cleaver, Chinese style. Arrange the duck pieces on a warmed serving dish, spoon the sweet potatoes and gravy over. Garnish with a vegetable flower.

Crisp-Fried Boneless Duck

Serves 6–8 as part of a meal
1 duckling, about 1.5 kg (3 lb)
1½ cups (12 fl oz) dark soy sauce
½ cup (4 fl oz) Chinese wine or dry sherry
2 whole star anise
2 cloves
2 sticks cinnamon
1 teaspoon fennel seeds
1 teaspoon Szechwan peppercorns
5 slices fresh ginger
2 tablespoons sugar
oil for deep frying
Batter:
1 cup (4 oz) self-raising flour
pinch of salt
For serving:
plum sauce
garnishes such as carrot or onion flowers

Place fried duck in pan with soy mixture.

Remove all bones from the duck.

Dip pieces of duck into batter before frying.

Wash and dry the duck well. Rub it all over with some of the dark soy sauce and set it aside for at least 30 minutes.

In a large saucepan combine the rest of the dark soy sauce with 1½ cups (12 fl oz) water, the wine and the spices which have been knotted in a square of muslin. Add ginger and sugar and bring to a gentle simmer.

Heat at least 5 cups of oil in a wok for deep frying the duck and when the oil is hot, slide the duck into it. Fry first one side and then the other until it is evenly brown all over.

Lift the duck out of the wok and put it into the saucepan containing the soy mixture. Bring to a simmer, turn the heat very low, cover the saucepan and cook for 1 hour or until the duck is tender when tested. Lift duck out of the sauce and drain in a colander. Allow duck to become cold enough to handle.

Meanwhile, make a thick batter with the self-raising flour, whisking until smooth with sufficient cold water to give a thick coating consistency. Let the batter stand for at least 1 hour.

Lay the duck on its back on a wooden board and, with a sharp chopper, cut through the skin of the duck, right down the middle. Find the breast bone, right below the neck, and wiggle it out. Spread the skin away from the bones as though unzipping a coat down the front. It is now quite easy to lift out the bony framework (use it for making stock).

Turn the duck over, breast downwards, and make slits in the legs and wings. Loosen the bones and coax them out, twisting them free at the joints. Turn duck over again, feel for the thigh bones and remove these as well.

Cut duck in half lengthways and chop the now-boneless duck crossways into strips 2.5 cm (1 inch) wide.

Reheat the oil for the second frying, but do not have it too hot. Dip the pieces of duck into the batter and then slide them into the oil, a few at a time. Spoon the oil over while cooking. When golden brown, lift them out and drain. When all the pieces are fried, place them on a serving platter and spoon plum sauce over. Finish with a bright garnish and serve with hot steamed rice or Mandarin Pancakes (see page 141).

Note: The liquid in which the duck simmered is now a Master Sauce and may be used for cooking other poultry, meat or seafood. Use a spoonful to give good flavour to sauces. It also freezes well.

Meat

In Chinese cuisine, meat is cut into thin slices or shreds so that it cooks quickly. Each piece is small enough not to require further cutting and knives are never used at the table. In the few dishes where meat is cooked in a large piece, it is sliced or diced after cooking and before serving, generally combined with other ingredients. No great piece of meat (as in the western roast) ever appears at the table.

Meat is synonymous with pork in China. Pigs are easy to raise, live on scraps and are within the means of most people.

Lamb is not favoured except in the northern provinces, since to the Chinese palate its flavour is too strong. In those dishes where it is used, there is no denying the skill of the chefs in giving it more pleasing flavour. The recipe for Mongolian Lamb is a perfect example.

Cattle are considered too valuable as working animals, and grazing land is scarce, so beef is not common in traditional Chinese dishes. But beef is readily available and popular in western countries, and here the Chinese chefs have adapted it to recipes which are a revelation in flavour and in illustrating how a little meat can go a long way.

Not every dish of exquisitely tender beef served at a Chinese meal is cut from the eye of the fillet – though its melting texture would indicate just that. There is a secret worth knowing. While rump and fillet must be used if there is no time to marinate it, cheaper cuts of lean meat may be used for stir-fried dishes if they are tenderized in this way.

Use round, blade or skirt steak, and freeze it until just firm enough to slice very thinly. For 500 g (1 lb) of meat, dissolve half a teaspoon of bicarbonate of soda (baking soda) in 3 tablespoons of water. Add this to the meat and knead well until liquid is absorbed. Refrigerate for at least 2 hours, or overnight if possible. Proceed with the recipe. If liked, other marinade ingredients may be added along with the tenderizing marinade. This method is used in many Chinese restaurants, making cheaper meat as tender as the choicest fillet.

Left: clockwise from front: lily buds; preserved cumquats; sliced chilli; Barbecued Pork (see page 110); Cold Steamed Lamb with Pungent Sauce (see page 121); barbecued pork spareribs; Clay Pot Beef (see page 104); lap cheong; fresh coriander; lotus root.

Clay Pot Beef

Drop the piece of beef into a pan of boiling water and simmer for 5 minutes. Rinse under cold water. Remove excess fat and gristle, and cut the meat into 1.5 cm (½ inch) slices.

Shake the peppercorns in a dry pan over low heat until they smell pungent. Grind to fine powder with a pestle and mortar.

Heat a wok, add 2 tablespoons of the oil and fry the meat until brown on all sides.

Place the meat in a clay pot or heatproof bowl and add the pepper, salt, sugar, ginger, garlic, wine, star anise and tangerine peel. Cover with a lid or foil, and place in a large steamer or boiler which contains water about 5 cm (2 inches) deep. Simmer for 2 hours, adding more boiling water as necessary.

Meanwhile, soak mushrooms in hot water to cover for 30 minutes. Drain, squeeze out water. Cut off and discard the mushroom stems and cut the caps into quarters. Cut the spring onions into three or four lengths, discarding some of the green top. Cut the Chinese cabbage into 5 cm (2 inch) lengths.

Heat a wok and add 1 tablespoon of the oil. Stir-fry the spring onions and mushrooms for 2 minutes. Then add the meat together with any liquid in the bowl. Remove the star anise and tangerine peel. Add the soy sauce and oyster sauce to the meat, cover the wok and simmer for 10 minutes.

Blanch the cabbage for 1 minute in boiling salted water to which the remaining tablespoon of oil has been added. Drain well and add to the meat. Serve with steamed rice.
Note: The finely peeled rind of 1 orange may be used instead of the dried tangerine peel.

Serves 6

1 kg (2 lb) brisket of beef
    or other stewing beef
1 teaspoon Szechwan
    peppercorns
4 tablespoons oil
½ teaspoon salt
2 teaspoons sugar
4 slices fresh ginger
2 cloves garlic, peeled
1 tablespoon Chinese wine
    or dry sherry
2 whole star anise
1 piece dried tangerine
    peel
5 dried Chinese
    mushrooms
6 spring onions (scallions)
3–4 stalks choy sum or
    other Chinese cabbage
1 tablespoon dark soy
    sauce
1 tablespoon oyster sauce

Place the beef in a clay pot with flavourings.

Cut choy sum into pieces.

Add meat and juices to stir-fried vegetables.

Beef in Black Bean Sauce

Serves 4
375 g (12 oz) lean rump or fillet steak
1 tablespoon canned salted black beans
1 large onion
1 head broccoli or 1 gai choy (Chinese mustard cabbage)
2 teaspoons cornflour (cornstarch)
3 tablespoons peanut oil
1 teaspoon crushed garlic
1 teaspoon finely grated fresh ginger
Sauce:
1 tablespoon dark soy sauce
⅓ cup water or stock
1 teaspoon sugar
1 teaspoon sesame oil

Cut the broccoli into bite-size pieces.

Cut partially frozen beef into paper-thin slices.

Trim any fat from the beef. Freeze the beef only until firm enough to cut into paper-thin slices. Use a very sharp knife for the slicing.

Put the black beans into a small strainer and rinse under cold water for a few seconds. Drain, and chop them on a wooden board or mash them with a fork.

Peel the onion, cut it in half lengthways and cut each half into six wedges. Cut the broccoli into bite-size pieces, keeping a bit of stem with each floweret; or slice the gai choy into thick pieces. Blanch the green vegetable for 1 minute in boiling salted water; drain.

Mix the cornflour with 1 tablespoon of cold water. In another bowl, combine the sauce ingredients.

Heat the wok until very hot, add 1 tablespoon of the peanut oil and swirl to coat the cooking surface. Stir-fry the onion for 1 minute. Remove the onion and set it aside with the green vegetables.

Add another tablespoon of peanut oil to the wok and when very hot, stir-fry the beef slices over high heat, tossing and stirring so that all the meat comes into contact with the hot pan and it loses its redness.

Push the meat to one side of the wok, heat the remaining tablespoon of peanut oil, add the garlic and ginger and stir for a few seconds until they smell fragrant. Add the black beans and fry, stirring, for a few seconds more. Toss with the meat, add the sauce mixture, reduce the heat and simmer for 2 minutes.

Add the cornflour mixture and stir until the sauce boils and thickens. Add the vegetables and toss together until heated through. Serve immediately with rice.

Seared Fillet Steak in Plum Sauce

Serves 4–6
500 g (1 lb) fillet steak
**2 tablespoons light soy
sauce**
**1 tablespoon Chinese wine
or dry sherry**
1 teaspoon grated ginger
1 teaspoon sugar
**1 clove garlic crushed in ½
teaspoon salt**
**1 bok choy (Chinese chard
cabbage)**
peanut oil for deep frying
½ teaspoon sugar
6 spring onions (scallions)
2 tablespoons oil
3 tablespoons plum sauce

Trim the beef, removing all fat and gristle. Cut into 1.5 cm (½ inch) slices. Press each slice of meat with the palm of your hand to flatten it slightly. Combine the soy sauce, wine, ginger, sugar and garlic. Add the beef and turn the slices to coat them. Leave to marinate for 1 hour or longer.

Meanwhile prepare the bok choy. Shred the green leaves of the cabbage very finely. Heat oil in a wok for deep frying and when hot, add the shredded cabbage. Scoop it out with a wire spoon almost immediately. Drain and sprinkle it with the sugar to keep crisp.

Cut the spring onions into 2.5 cm (1 inch) lengths.

Heat a wok, add 1 tablespoon of the oil and when hot, fry half of the beef, pressing the slices against the wok and turning to brown both sides. Remove and set aside. Add the remaining tablespoon of oil to the wok and when hot, cook the remaining beef. Add the spring onions and first lot of meat and toss together.

Stir in plum sauce and 1 tablespoon of water. Cook for about 1 minute until thoroughly heated. Serve on a bed of crisp-fried bok choy.

Cut beef into thick slices.

Briefly fry bok choy until crisp.

Slice spring onions diagonally.

Shredded Beef with Asparagus

Serves 3–4

375 g (12 oz) round or other lean steak
½ teaspoon bicarbonate of soda (baking soda)
2 onions
1 bunch asparagus
4 tablespoons peanut oil
Marinade:
2 teaspoons dark soy sauce
2 teaspoons cornflour (cornstarch)
½ teaspoon sugar
1 tablespoon Chinese wine or dry sherry
Sauce:
1 tablespoon light soy sauce
1 tablespoon oyster sauce
1 tablespoon water
2 teaspoons cornflour (cornstarch)

Cut the meat into fine shreds, discarding any fat. Dissolve the bicarbonate of soda in 3 tablespoons of water, pour this over the meat and knead well until the meat absorbs the liquid. Refrigerate for 2 hours or longer if possible. This tenderizes economical cuts of meat. If time is short, use a tender cut of beef and omit this step.

Peel the onions and cut them in half lengthways, then cut each half into six wedges. Snap off any tough ends of asparagus and discard; cut the stalks into 5 cm (2 inch) lengths.

Combine the marinade ingredients, add to the meat and mix well. Leave to marinate for about 20 minutes. In a small bowl, mix the sauce ingredients.

Heat a wok, add 1 tablespoon of the peanut oil and stir-fry the onions over high heat for 1 minute. Remove the onions to a plate.

Add 2 tablespoons of peanut oil to the wok and when very hot, add the meat and toss over high heat until its colour changes. Put the meat aside with the onions.

Wipe out the wok and heat the remaining tablespoon of peanut oil. Stir-fry the asparagus for 1 minute. Then add ¼ cup (2 fl oz) hot water, cover the wok and cook for 3 minutes or until the asparagus is tender but still crisp.

Add the sauce ingredients and stir until boiling and slightly thickened. Then return the beef and onions to the wok and toss together until heated through. Serve hot.

Snap off ends of asparagus.

Stir-fry shredded beef until it changes colour.

Add hot water to stir-fried asparagus.

Chilli Beef with Bitter Melon

Bitter melon

Halve bitter melon and scoop out spongy centre.

Rinse black beans under cold water.

Remove any fat from the meat and slice the meat thinly across the grain. Dissolve the bicarbonate of soda in 2 tablespoons of hot water. Add to the meat and knead well until the meat absorbs all the liquid. Cover and refrigerate for 2 hours or longer.

Halve the bitter melon lengthways. Scoop out and discard the spongy centre and seeds. Cut the melon into 12 mm (½ inch) slices. Sprinkle 1 teaspoon of salt over the melon pieces and lightly mix through. Leave for 30 minutes or longer.

Rinse the melon pieces under a cold tap, and drain. Rinse the black beans under cold water, drain, and chop. Combine the soy sauce, chilli bean sauce, sugar and cornflour with 4 tablespoons of water.

Heat the wok, add 2 tablespoons of the oil and when hot, add the beef and stir-fry over high heat, tossing and stirring until brown. Remove to a plate.

Add 1 more tablespoon of oil to the wok and when hot, stir-fry the bitter melon for 2 minutes. Remove.

Heat the remaining oil, add garlic and stir-fry for a few seconds. Add black beans and fry, stirring for a few seconds more. Stir the sauce mixture, add it to the wok and stir until it boils and thickens. Return the melon to the wok, simmer for 5 minutes. Then stir in the beef until reheated through. Serve immediately, garnished with chilli flowers.

Serves 4

375 g (12 oz) round or skirt (flank) steak
½ teaspoon bicarbonate of soda (baking soda)
1 large bitter melon
1 teaspoon salt
1 tablespoon canned salted black beans
1 tablespoon dark soy sauce
2 teaspoons chilli bean sauce
1 teaspoon sugar
1 teaspoon cornflour (cornstarch)
5 tablespoons peanut oil
1 teaspoon crushed garlic

Stir-Fried Beef with Capsicums

Serves 4–6

500 g (1 lb) beef fillet or
    rump
1 clove garlic
1 teaspoon salt
1 teaspoon finely grated
    fresh ginger
½ teaspoon five spice
    powder
1 large red pepper
    (capsicum)
1 large green pepper
    (capsicum)
2 teaspoons cornflour
    (cornstarch)
4 tablespoons cold water
2 tablespoons dark soy
    sauce
2 teaspoons sesame oil
2 tablespoons peanut oil
3 or 4 spring onions
    (scallions) for garnish

Trim off all fat from the beef. Place it in the freezer for about 2 hours, long enough to make it firm, not hard. This makes it easy to cut into paper-thin slices.

Crush garlic with salt, and rub into beef with the ginger and five spice, mixing well.

Remove stem, seeds and membranes from the red and green peppers (capsicums) and cut into thin slices. In a small bowl, mix the cornflour, water, soy sauce and sesame oil together.

Heat a wok and when hot, add 1 tablespoon of the peanut oil and heat for a further 30 seconds. Swirl the wok to coat its inner surface. Add the capsicum strips and stir-fry over high heat for 1 minute. Remove from wok.

Add the remaining tablespoon of peanut oil and heat again, then add the beef and fry over high heat for 2 minutes, stirring constantly, until the beef changes colour. Add the cornflour mixture and stir until it boils and thickens. Then return the capsicum strips to the wok and combine with beef.

Serve immediately accompanied by rice or noodles. Garnish, if desired, with spring onion flowers.

Slice partially frozen beef thinly.

Barbecued Pork

Special barrel-shaped ovens are used to cook this popular item. This recipe gives two ways to get almost the same effect in your own oven at home.

CUT THE PORK lengthways into three or four strips. Crush the garlic with the salt and combine with all the remaining ingredients in a large bowl. Add the pork and mix well together so that the meat is covered on all sides with the mixture. Allow it to marinate for 15 minutes or longer if convenient.

For the first cooking method, the pork is hung in strips from the top rack in the oven. To make suitable hooks, cut lengths of wire 10 cm (4 inches) long from wire coat-hangers using pliers or wire cutters. Shape each end into an 'S' shape, the top hook smaller than the base which holds the pork.

Remove all racks from oven except one, which should be on the highest level. Put a roasting pan with a little water in it on the bottom shelf.

Preheat the oven to 200°C (400°F/Gas 6). Insert a metal hook in the end of each strip of pork and hang it from the rack. Roast for 15 minutes in the hot oven, then reduce the temperature to 190°C (375°F/Gas 5), brush the meat with the marinade and continue roasting for a further 30 minutes or until the pork is cooked.

Remove from oven, allow to cool for at least 10 minutes, then cut in thin slices crossways.

The second method of cooking is to half-fill a roasting pan with hot water and put a wire rack across the top of the pan. Place the strips of pork on the rack (reserving the marinade) and roast in an oven preheated to 200°C (400°F/Gas 6) for 15 minutes, then turn the pork, brush with marinade and continue roasting for 15 minutes. Turn the meat again and baste it, and roast for another 15 minutes or until the pork is tender and well glazed.

Barbecued pork may be served hot or cold as an hors d'oeuvre or part of a meal, or the meat can be used in other dishes such as fried rice. Stir-fried with snow peas or fresh green beans, it makes a quick, light meal. On its own, serve with plum sauce and steamed bread.

Thread pork on wire hooks.

To cook, hang from shelf in oven.

Or place the strips on a wire rack in a roasting pan.

Serves 4–6
1 kg (2 lb) pork neck or boneless loin
1 teaspoon finely chopped garlic
1 teaspoon salt
½ teaspoon finely grated fresh ginger
2 tablespoons dark soy sauce
2 tablespoons honey
1 tablespoon Chinese wine or dry sherry
½ teaspoon five spice powder
1 tablespoon hoi sin sauce

Stir-Fried Garlic Beef and Gai Choy

Remove any fat from the meat. Slice the meat thinly across the grain.

In a bowl, dissolve the bicarbonate of soda in 4 table-spoons of water. Add the sugar, cornflour and sliced meat and knead the liquid well into the meat until the liquid is absorbed. Refrigerate for 2 hours or overnight.

Soak the mushrooms in hot water for 30 minutes. Discard the mushroom stems, and cut the caps into halves (or quarters, if large).

Wash the cabbage and drain it well, then slice diagonally, discarding any tough ends of outer leaves.

Crush the garlic in the salt. Combine the ingredients for the sauce in a small bowl.

Heat a wok, add 2 tablespoons of the peanut oil and swirl the wok to coat its sides. Add beef and stir-fry over high heat until the meat's colour changes. Remove to a plate.

Add the remaining tablespoon of peanut oil to the wok. When hot add the cabbage, garlic and mushrooms, and stir-fry for 1 minute. Then return the meat to the wok and continue to cook for 30 seconds. Add the sauce mixture and stir through. Turn off the heat and stir in the sesame oil. Serve immediately with boiled rice.

Serves 3–4
375 g (12 oz) skirt (flank) steak
½ teaspoon bicarbonate of soda (baking soda)
1 teaspoon sugar
1 teaspoon cornflour (cornstarch)
6–8 dried Chinese mushrooms
1 small bunch gai choy (mustard cabbage), about 250 g (8 oz)
4 cloves garlic
1 teaspoon salt
3 tablespoons peanut oil
2 teaspoons sesame oil
Sauce:
1 tablespoon Chinese wine or dry sherry
1 tablespoon dark soy sauce
2 tablespoons oyster sauce

Work the bicarbonate of soda mixture into the meat to tenderize.

Crush the garlic with salt.

Stir-fry cabbage, garlic and mushrooms.

Braised Pork Spareribs with Smoked Mussels

Serves 4–6

750 g (1½ lb) pork
spareribs
2 cloves garlic, crushed
1 tablespoon light soy
sauce
1 tablespoon Chinese wine
or dry sherry
½ teaspoon salt
2 tablespoons peanut oil
2 cups (16 fl oz) hot stock
or water
125 g (4 oz) smoked
mussels
3 teaspoons cornflour
(cornstarch)

Cut the spareribs into chunky pieces. Mix together the garlic, soy sauce, wine and salt, and marinate the spareribs in this mixture for at least 30 minutes.

Heat a wok and when very hot, add the oil and swirl to coat the surface. On high heat, fry the spareribs, tossing to brown all surfaces. Turn the heat to low, add the hot stock (or water) and 2 or 3 mussels to give a pronounced smoky flavour. Cover the wok and simmer for 45 minutes or until the pork is tender and the liquid reduced.

Add the remaining mussels and cook for a further 10 minutes.

Blend the cornflour smoothly with 1 tablespoon of cold water, add this to the wok and stir constantly until the sauce boils and thickens. Serve hot with rice.

Cut spareribs into chunky pieces.

Add mussels to spareribs.

Mu Shu Pork

Serves 4

250 g (8 oz) boneless lean
  pork
2 teaspoons light soy sauce
2 teaspoons Chinese wine
  or dry sherry
2 teaspoons cornflour
  (cornstarch)
4 dried Chinese
  mushrooms
30 dried lily buds
2 tablespoons dried wood
  fungus
1 piece canned winter
  bamboo shoot
2 spring onions (scallions)
1 whole egg and 1 egg yolk
¼ teaspoon salt

3 tablespoons peanut oil
1 teaspoon sesame oil
Sauce:
1 tablespoon oyster sauce
1 tablespoon Chinese wine
  or dry sherry
1 tablespoon light soy
  sauce
For serving:
hoi sin or sweet chilli
  sauce
spring onion 'brushes'
Mandarin Pancakes (see
  page 141), or Silver
  Thread Rolls (page 142),
  or Flower Rolls (page
  143)

Fun to eat, this is something you use your fingers for like Crisp Fried Boneless Duck or Lettuce Rolls. Brush each pancake with hoi sin or sweet chilli sauce, top with some pork filling, roll up and enjoy. Serve as a first course or a complete light luncheon.

PARTIALLY FREEZE THE PORK until it is firm enough to cut into very thin slices, then into shreds. Use a very sharp knife for slicing. Mix with the soy sauce, wine and 1 teaspoon of the cornflour. Refrigerate for at least 30 minutes.

Meanwhile, put the dried mushrooms and lily buds into a bowl, pour very hot water to cover them, and soak for 30 minutes. Then drain, discard the mushroom stems and cut the mushroom caps into thin strips. Discard the hard tips of the lily buds and tie each bud into a knot.

Soak the wood fungus in cold water for 10 minutes. Drain, pinch off any hard, gritty portions and cut the shapes into smaller pieces.

Shred the bamboo shoot into matchstick strips. Finely slice the spring onions. Combine the sauce ingredients with 3 tablespoons of water. Beat the egg and yolk together with the salt.

Heat a wok, add 1 tablespoon of the peanut oil and pour in the beaten egg. Swirl the pan, then stir and cook until the egg is firm without browning. Remove from heat and cut into small pieces with a wok chan. Immediately turn out onto a dish. Wipe the wok with paper.

Reheat the wok, add another tablespoon of peanut oil and stir-fry the bamboo shoot and spring onions on high heat for 1 minute. Remove to plate.

Heat the remaining tablespoon of peanut oil. On high heat, stir-fry the pork, mushrooms and lily buds until the pork changes colour. Add the sauce mixture, cover the wok and cook for 3 minutes. Mix the remaining teaspoon of cornflour with 1 tablespoon of cold water and stir into the sauce until it boils and thickens.

Return the spring onions and bamboo shoot to the wok, together with the wood fungus. Drizzle the sesame oil over and stir rapidly together. Remove from heat and fold in the cooked egg.

Serve hot with spring onion brushes and either Mandarin Pancakes, Silver Thread Rolls, or Flower Rolls.

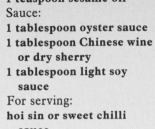

Cut pork into shreds.

Tie lily buds into knots.

Stir-Fried Pork with Walnuts and Lotus Root

Thinly slice partially frozen pork.

Slice lotus root.

Walnut skins lift off easily after boiling.

Serves 4

375 g (12 oz) pork fillet or schnitzel
2 teaspoons light soy sauce
1 teaspoon Chinese wine or dry sherry
½ teaspoon salt
½ teaspoon crushed garlic
½ teaspoon finely grated fresh ginger
1 canned lotus root
½ cup (60 g or 2 oz) peeled walnut halves
oil for frying
2 teaspoons cornflour (cornstarch)
Sauce:
½ cup (4 fl oz) stock or water
2 teaspoons oyster sauce
1 tablespoon Chinese wine or dry sherry
1 teaspoon sesame oil
1 teaspoon chilli oil (optional)

Freeze the pork until it is firm enough to cut into paper-thin slices. Use a very sharp knife for the slicing.

Combine the soy sauce, wine, salt, garlic, and ginger in a bowl. Add the sliced pork, mix well and leave to marinate.

Slice the lotus root thinly and set aside. Peeled walnuts are not always easy to find, but it is better to remove the fine skin as this becomes bitter when the walnuts are fried. Here is an easy way to do this. Bring a small pan of water to the boil, add the walnut halves and simmer for 7 minutes. Drain, then spread on kitchen paper. The thin skin may be peeled off easily.

Heat about 1 cup (8 fl oz) oil in a wok and deep fry the nuts on low heat, stirring and turning them constantly, just until golden brown (this should take less than a minute). Drain on absorbent paper.

Mix all the sauce ingredients together.

Reheat the wok, add 1 tablespoon of oil and swirl to coat the wok. When the oil is very hot, add the marinated pork mixture and stir-fry on high heat until the pork is browned. Add the sauce mixture and when it boils lower the heat, cover the wok and simmer for 5 minutes.

Blend the cornflour with 1 tablespoon of cold water, stir this into the pork mixture. When the sauce boils and thickens slightly, add the lotus root and heat through. Arrange on a dish and sprinkle the walnut halves over. Garnish with cucumber.

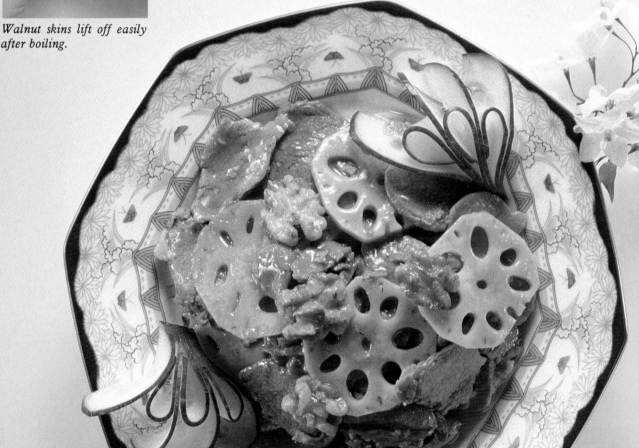

Pork with Sweet Cumquats

Serves 4

375 g (12 oz) pork fillet or lean pork chops
1 tablespoon Chinese wine or dry sherry
1 tablespoon light soy sauce
1 teaspoon grated fresh ginger
1 tablespoon cornflour (cornstarch)
3 spring onions (scallions)
peanut oil for deep frying
8 sweet cumquats preserved in syrup

Sauce:
2 tablespoons Chinese wine or dry sherry
1 tablespoon sugar
1 tablespoon light soy sauce
2 tablespoons white vinegar
1 tablespoon cumquat syrup
1 teaspoon cornflour (cornstarch)

Cut the pork into small squares. Marinate in wine, soy sauce and ginger for 20 minutes.

Stir the cornflour into the pork and marinade. Cut the spring onions diagonally into short lengths. Combine the sauce ingredients with 1 tablespoon of water.

Heat a wok, add oil for deep frying and when hot, fry the pork in three or four batches until brown and cooked through. Drain. Pour the oil from the wok into a heat-proof bowl and reserve for future use.

Return 1 tablespoon of the oil to the wok and gently cook the spring onions. Add the pork and sauce mixture, stirring constantly until heated through. Lastly stir in the cumquats. Serve immediately on a bed of Stir-Fried Lettuce (see page 49).

Cumquats in syrup.

Cut the pork into pieces.

Deep fry the pork in 3 or 4 batches.

Braised Honey Pork

Serves 6

1 kg (2 lb) boneless loin of pork

1 tablespoon canned black beans

1 teaspoon crushed garlic

1 teaspoon salt

2 teaspoons finely grated fresh ginger

2 tablespoons honey

2 tablespoons Chinese wine or dry sherry

½ teaspoon five spice powder

3 tablespoons dark soy sauce

2 tablespoons peanut oil

Ask the butcher to remove rind from the pork. Cut the pork into strips 5 cm × 2.5 cm (2 inches × 1 inch).

Wash the black beans well under running cold water. Drain and chop. Combine all ingredients except the peanut oil and mix with the pork. Leave for at least 15 minutes to marinate.

Heat a wok, add the peanut oil and swirl to coat the wok. Add the pork pieces (reserving the marinade) and stir-fry until they are browned. Then add the reserved marinade. Swirl ¾ cup (6 fl oz) hot water in the marinating bowl and add that too.

Reduce the heat, cover the wok and simmer for 30 to 40 minutes until pork is tender. Stir occasionally and add more hot water if the liquid seems to be drying up. Be careful that the sweet marinade does not burn. The heat should be very low throughout the cooking.

When the pork is tender, remove from heat. If it is not to be served straightaway, it may be reheated at serving time. Serve on a bed of Braised Chinese Cabbage (see page 48) with plain rice and garnish with coriander.

Cut the pork into strips.

Stir-fry the marinated pork until brown.

Spicy Pork Spareribs

Serves 6–8

- 1.5 kg (3 lb) pork spareribs
- 1½ teaspoons crushed garlic
- 1 teaspoon sugar
- 1 teaspoon finely grated fresh ginger
- 2 tablespoons dark soy sauce
- 1 tablespoon hoi sin sauce
- 2 teaspoons sesame sauce
- 1 tablespoon honey
- 1–2 teaspoons chilli sauce (optional)
- 1 tablespoon Chinese wine or dry sherry

Ask the butcher to cut rack of bones into lengths of four or five bones each. At home, use a sharp knife to cut between the bones, but do not separate them.

Crush the garlic with the sugar and combine with all the remaining ingredients in a large bowl. Beat well with a spoon to mix together. The sesame sauce should be stirred well in its jar before measuring the required amount, because the oil will have floated to the top and the paste will be settled at the bottom. Pour the marinade over the pork and rub it in on all sides and between the bones. Marinate for 1 hour or more.

Preheat the oven to 200°C (400°F/Gas 6). Place a rack in a roasting pan (or across the top) and pour some hot water into the pan; water should not touch the rack. Place the marinated spareribs on the rack. Cook in the hot oven for 20 minutes, then reduce the temperature to 180°C (350°F/Gas 4), turn the ribs over and cook for a further 25 minutes or longer.

When ready, the spareribs should be reddish-brown all over, touched with dark brown here and there as if barbecued over open coals. Depending on thickness of the spareribs, the total cooking time may be between 45 minutes and 1 hour. Cut into pieces to serve and garnish with tomato roses and coriander.

This dish can be cooked ahead and reheated under the griller.

Note: The spareribs can also be cooked in a frying pan. Heat 1–2 tablespoons of peanut oil in a large, heavy frying pan and brown them. Add ½ cup (4 fl oz) hot water, cover the frying pan and simmer for 30 to 35 minutes or until tender. Then cook, uncovered, until liquid evaporates and the ribs look glazed.

Make cuts between the ribs.

Rub marinade over ribs.

Place ribs on a rack over water for baking.

Stir-Fried Lamb with Chilli and Garlic

Add lamb to soy mixture.

Slice water chestnuts.

Garlic is combined with chilli bean sauce.

Serves 6

500 g (1 lb) leg lamb chops
(or shoulder chops)
1 tablespoon light soy
sauce
2 teaspoons grated fresh
ginger
2 teaspoons cornflour
(cornstarch)
1 tablespoon Chinese wine
or dry sherry
1 teaspoon sugar
3 spring onions (scallions)
1 × 230 g (7½ oz) can water
chestnuts
125 g (4 oz) snow peas
2 teaspoons crushed garlic
2 teaspoons chilli bean
sauce
4 tablespoons peanut oil
Sauce:
2 tablespoons dark soy
sauce
1 tablespoon sugar
1 tablespoon Chinese wine
or dry sherry
2 teaspoons cornflour
(cornstarch)
2 teaspoons Chinese black
vinegar
3 tablespoons water

Trim and discard the skin, fat and bones from the chops. Cut the meat into strips. Combine the soy sauce, ginger, cornflour, wine and sugar. Add the lamb strips and mix well. Leave to marinate for 30 minutes.

Finely chop the spring onions. Drain the water chestnuts and halve them. Combine the sauce ingredients in a small bowl. String and wash the snow peas. Combine the garlic and the chilli bean sauce.

Heat a wok until very hot. Add 3 tablespoons of the peanut oil and swirl to coat the wok. Add the lamb and stir-fry over high heat until the meat changes colour. Add the spring onion, water chestnuts and snow peas, and fry for about 30 seconds.

Push the meat and vegetables to one side of the wok, add the remaining tablespoon of peanut oil in the centre, and fry the garlic and chilli bean sauce, stirring, for a few seconds until it smells fragrant.

Stir the sauce ingredients again because the cornflour will have settled at the bottom, add this to the wok and stir until the sauce is thick and clear. Toss the meat and vegetables in the sauce, and serve at once. Garnish with sliced cucumber and onion flowers.

Sesame Lamb on Crisp Noodles

Trim all the fat from the lamb and remove the bones. Cut the meat into very thin slices. Mix with the sugar, salt and soy sauce. Leave for 10 minutes.

Add the egg white, 1 tablespoon of peanut oil and the cornflour. Mix well and chill for 30 minutes.

Cut the spring onions into bite-sized pieces. Slice the capsicum into strips.

Heat a wok, add 2 tablespoons of peanut oil. When hot, add the garlic, spring onions and capsicum, and stir-fry for 10 seconds. Then add the meat and stir-fry until its colour changes. Remove and set aside.

Add all ingredients for the sauce to the wok, add 3 tablespoons of water and stir over low heat until it is smooth. Return the lamb and vegetables to the wok and stir until heated. Serve on a bed of fried noodles.

To prepare the noodles: Heat 1½ cups of peanut oil in a wok and when hot, add about one-quarter of the noodles at a time. They will puff and turn white instantly. Drain on paper towels. They may be done beforehand, but store them in an airtight container until served.

Serves 4

500 g (1 lb) lean lamb chops
1 teaspoon sugar
½ teaspoon salt
1 tablespoon light soy sauce
1 egg white
peanut oil
2 teaspoons cornflour (cornstarch)
3 spring onions (scallions)
1 small red capsicum (red pepper)
½ teaspoon crushed garlic
60 g (2 oz) transparent noodles or rice vermicelli

Sauce:
2 heaped teaspoons sesame sauce
2 tablespoons dark soy sauce
2 tablespoons Chinese wine or dry sherry
1 teaspoon sugar
½ teaspoon chilli oil (optional)

Stir-fry garlic, spring onions, capsicum and lamb.

The transparent noodles.

Noodles puff and turn white instantly when fried.

Mongolian Lamb

Serves 4

500 g (1 lb) boned leg of lamb
2 teaspoons sugar
1 teaspoon salt
2 tablespoons dark soy sauce
1 small egg, beaten
½ teaspoon bicarbonate of soda (baking soda)
2 teaspoons cornflour (cornstarch)
4 tablespoons peanut oil
1 large onion cut in wedges lengthways
1 spring onion (scallion), finely sliced
1 teaspoon finely chopped garlic
Sauce:
¼ teaspoon five spice powder
1 tablespoon hoi sin sauce
1 tablespoon ground bean sauce (mor sze jeung)
1 teaspoon chilli bean sauce
1 tablespoon Chinese wine or dry sherry

The process of soaking, rinsing and marinating lessens the strong flavour of lamb, which is not popular in China except in the North. It also tenderizes the meat. This recipe uses about half a small leg of lamb – the rest may be used for another dish or frozen.

TRIM AWAY ANY FAT, skin and gristle from the meat. Freeze the meat until firm, then cut into bite-size, paper-thin slices. Soak in cold water for 30 minutes. Rinse under a cold tap until water runs clear, then drain well and squeeze out excess water.

Combine the sugar, salt, soy sauce, egg, bicarbonate of soda and cornflour. Add the meat and mix well. Add 1 tablespoon of the peanut oil and mix again. Leave to marinate for at least 2 hours.

Heat a wok, add 1 tablespoon of the peanut oil and, on medium-high heat, stir-fry the onion wedges and spring onion for 1 minute. Remove from the wok.

Add the remaining 2 tablespoons of peanut oil to the wok, heat the oil and swirl to coat the cooking surface. Fry the garlic for 5 seconds. Then add the lamb and stir-fry on high heat, tossing the meat constantly until it is brown. Add sauce ingredients except the wine, and toss again. Return the onion and spring onion to the wok. Add the wine, pouring it down the sides of the wok so that it sizzles. Mix, and serve at once with rice.

Note: Mongolian lamb is usually cooked on a flat griddle but can be done in the wok. A popular way of presenting this dish is on a heated sizzle plate brought to the table.

Slice partially frozen lamb thinly.

Cut onions lengthways into wedges.

Cold Steamed Lamb with Pungent Sauce

Ask the butcher to bone the lamb shoulder, but not roll the meat.

Combine the bean sauce, soy sauce, spring onions, garlic, ginger, star anise broken into pieces, wine, sugar and bean curd. Place the lamb in a bowl that will fit in your steamer, pour the sauce mixture over the lamb and rub it well into the meat. Leave for 30 minutes.

Cover and steam for 1½ hours, adding more boiling water to the steamer to replace the water that boils away.

Pour the liquid from the lamb into a saucepan and simmer until reduced and syrupy. Pour it over the lamb and chill.

To serve, cut the meat into thin slices and arrange them on a platter. It may be served as a part of an hors d'oeuvre selection, or as a cold meat dish accompanied by warm Silver Thread Rolls (see page 142) or Flower Rolls (see page 143).

Note: This dish is also delicious hot. If serving hot, lift the lamb out of the steamer and slice it. Reduce the sauce by quick cooking, then spoon it over the lamb, and serve.

Serves 6

- 1.2 kg (2½ lb) lamb shoulder, boned
- 1 tablespoon smooth bean sauce (mor sze jeung)
- 2 tablespoons dark soy sauce
- 2 spring onions (scallions) chopped
- 1 teaspoon finely grated garlic
- 1 teaspoon finely grated fresh ginger
- 1 star anise
- 1 tablespoon Chinese wine or dry sherry
- 1 tablespoon sugar
- 1 teaspoon red bean curd

The smooth bean sauce (mor sze jeung).

Break star anise into pieces.

Place marinated lamb into steamer for cooking.

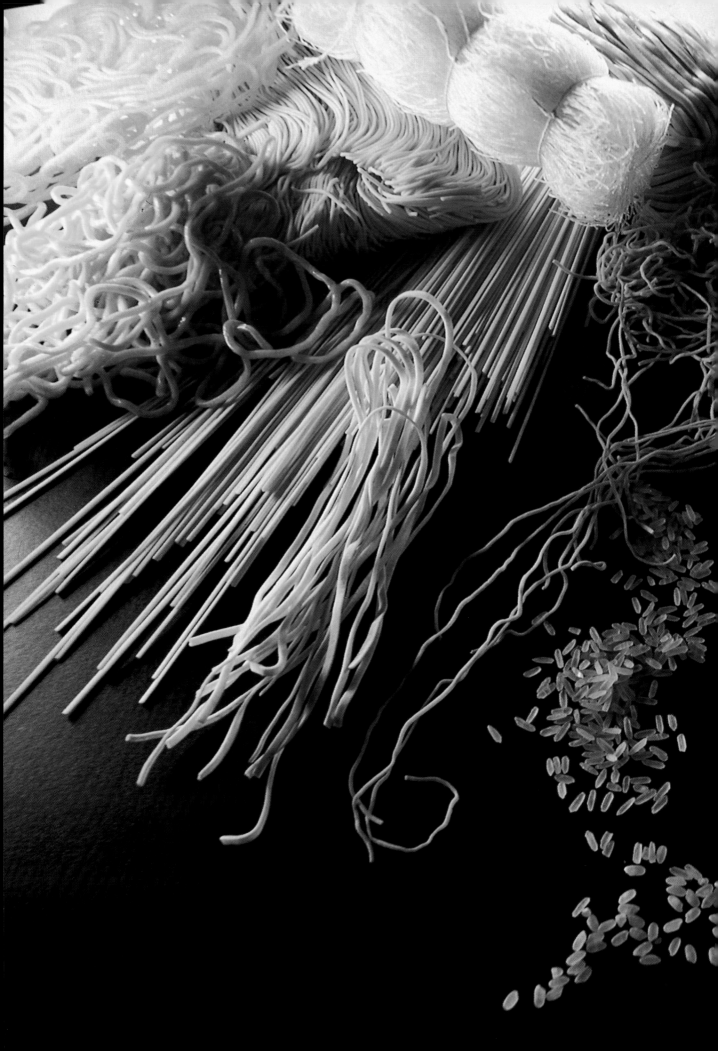

Rice and Noodles

Whatever else is on the table, rice or noodles are what fill the gaps. No Chinese meal is complete without one or the other, or both.

In the west we have been taught to expect well-cooked rice to be fluffy, so most restaurants serve long-grain rice which gives this result. To most Chinese, however, the medium grain is preferable. When correctly cooked, it is not fluffy but certainly not gluey. Each perfectly cooked grain is pearly and well defined, clinging in friendly fashion to neighbouring grains. Thus it is much easier to pick up with chopsticks, although the shovelling method (bowl held close to the mouth, and chopsticks working furiously) is also perfectly acceptable around the Chinese table.

Short and long-grain rice are not interchangeable in recipes, because the absorption rates are different (long-grain rice requiring more water).

It is not necessary to wash the clean rice sold in most western countries unless there is a lot of loose starch. If washing rice, drain it well or allow for the water retained when measuring the amount it is to be cooked in. The other type of rice sold in Chinese stores, glutinous rice, is used only for moulded snacks or for sweets.

In the north of China where wheat grows more readily, noodles, buns and pancakes take the place of rice. In the south, they make noodles from rice flour.

Left: clockwise from top left: Hokkien noodles; egg noodles; bundle of bean starch noodles; cellophane noodles; bundles of egg noodles; rice vermicelli; twin rice noodles; rice.

Chinese-Style Steamed Rice

Short or medium-grain rice is most used in China, but in western countries long-grain rice is popular. If using long-grain rice, increase the water to 3½ cups (28 fl oz) for 500 g rice as it has a greater absorbency.

If you buy rice in bulk, measure out 2½ cups, which is equivalent to 500 g. Wash the rice and drain well, then put the measured water (hot or cold, it does not matter) into a saucepan with the rice.

Bring to the boil over high heat, and boil rapidly for 1 minute. Then reduce the heat to medium, and cook uncovered for 2 to 3 minutes, until holes appear in the rice mass and the surface looks dimpled. Do not stir.

Cover the saucepan with a well-fitting lid, reduce the heat to as low as possible and cook for a further 10 minutes. Without removing the lid, turn off the heat and let the rice sit undisturbed for a further 10 minutes.

Grains will be well defined and separate, but will cling together instead of being fluffy. This makes it easy to eat with chopsticks.

Cook rice, uncovered, until holes appear in the rice mass.

Serves 6

500 g (1 lb) medium-grain rice
3 cups (24 fl oz) water

Vegetarian Fried Rice

Use a mixture of colourful and crisp vegetables in season, diced or finely sliced – green beans, carrots, celery, zucchini (courgettes), cabbage, broccoli, cooked or frozen peas. Always include spring onions (scallions) with their green tops for flavour.

For a more elaborate non-vegetarian version, add diced cooked pork or chicken, steamed and sliced lap cheong, cooked and shelled prawns, chopped ham or bacon. Fry before combining with the vegetables and rice. The bean curd may be omitted.

COOK THE RICE, then spread it on a lightly oiled baking tray to cool; chill overnight if possible. Dice the bean curd. Lightly beat the eggs, with salt and pepper to taste.

Heat wok, add 1 tablespoon of peanut oil; swirl. Pour in the egg mixture, and stir until it is firm. Cut the egg into small pieces with a wok chan then remove from the wok and set aside.

Heat the remaining 3 tablespoons of oil and when hot, add the spring onions, garlic and ginger. Fry, stirring, for a few seconds until they smell fragrant. Add bean curd and stir-fry for 1 minute. Add vegetables and stir-fry for a further 1-2 minutes until the vegetables are tender but still crisp.

Add rice; stir and toss to heat through. Sprinkle soy sauce and sesame oil over, and add the coriander and cooked egg. Toss to mix, and serve immediately. Garnish with spring onion curls.

Cut cooked egg with wok chan.

Add rice to vegetables in wok, toss to heat through.

Serves 4–6

4 cups cooked rice, chilled (1½ cups raw rice)
2 squares pressed bean curd
2 eggs, lightly beaten
salt and pepper, to taste
4 tablespoons peanut oil
3 spring onions, finely chopped
1 teaspoon finely chopped garlic
1 teaspoon finely grated fresh ginger
1 tablespoon dark soy sauce
2 cups diced mixed vegetables
1 teaspoon sesame oil
3 tablespoons fresh coriander leaves, coarsely chopped
spring onion (scallion) 'curls' for garnishing.

Sizzling Rice with Sweet and Sour Seafood

Pouring a hot sauce over freshly fried rice cakes makes them hiss and sizzle, and this is altogether a most colourful and entertaining dish. The rice cakes may be made a day or two ahead and stored in an airtight container, then fried just before serving.

PUT THE RICE into a large saucepan about 25 cm (10 inches) in diameter, add 1½ cups (12 fl oz) water and bring to the boil. Boil uncovered until there is no visible liquid when pan is tilted and the surface of the rice looks dimpled; do not stir the rice at all. Turn the heat very low, cover the saucepan and cook for a further 15 minutes. Remove from heat and allow to cool.

Lift the rice out of the saucepan with a spatula. Place it on an oiled oven tray and press it with the heel of your hand to flatten it. Place in a preheated oven at 160°C (325°F/Gas 3) for 30 minutes or until dry and the edge feels crisp when touched. Remove from oven, allow to cool, then break it into pieces roughly 5 cm (2 inches) square.

Peel and de-vein the prawns, or if using scallops remove any brown veins. Rinse and dry them thoroughly, and place in a bowl. Sprinkle with salt, add the egg white, and mix through. Sprinkle cornflour and oil over, and mix again. Chill for 30 minutes at least.

Dice the capsicum, cut the spring onions into short lengths, thaw the peas, and slice the water chestnuts. All this may be done hours ahead.

Prepare the sauce. Put the tomato sauce, vinegar, soy sauce, wine and sugar into a saucepan; add ¾ cup (6 fl oz) water, and stir over heat to dissolve the sugar. Blend the cornflour with 3 tablespoons of cold water, add it to the sauce and stir until mixture boils and thickens. Keep warm.

Heat a wok, add about 3 cups of peanut oil and when hot, add the prawns (or scallops), stirring gently, until they turn pink. Drain at once, pouring through a wire strainer into a heatproof bowl. This oil can be used later for frying the rice cakes.

Return the wok to the heat, add 2 tablespoons of oil, and when hot, add the capsicum and stir-fry for 1 minute. Add spring onions, ginger and garlic and fry for 10 seconds or until fragrant. Add the peas and water chestnuts. Stir all the vegetables into the warm sauce.

Wipe out the wok, return to heat and once more heat the peanut oil for deep frying. When the oil is very hot, fry the rice cakes until crisp and golden. Drain and place in a serving bowl.

Reheat the sauce to boiling, add the prawns, and pour into a heated bowl. Quickly take both bowls to the table and pour the hot sauce over the hot rice cakes so they sizzle and steam. Serve at once into individual bowls, so that the rice cakes will still be crisp when eaten.

Serves 6 with other dishes
1 cup short-grain rice
500 g (1 lb) small raw prawns or scallops
½ teaspoon salt
1 egg white
3 teaspoons cornflour (cornstarch)
1 tablespoon peanut oil
1 red capsicum (sweet pepper)
3 or 4 spring onions (scallions)
4 tablespoons frozen peas
10 water chestnuts
½ teaspoon finely grated fresh ginger
½ teaspoon crushed garlic
3 cups (24 fl oz) peanut oil for deep frying
Sauce:
3 tablespoons tomato sauce
2 tablespoons white vinegar
1 tablespoon light soy sauce
1 tablespoon Chinese wine or dry sherry
3 tablespoons sugar
1 tablespoon cornflour (cornstarch)

Flatten cooked rice with heel of hand.

Break rice into pieces.

Deep fry rice until golden.

Rice Congee

This is a thin porridge or gruel made by simmering rice with water – the traditional Chinese breakfast. It is filling and easily digested, and can be made interesting and delicious when other ingredients are added, such as chicken, fish, pork, abalone, egg, frogs' legs. A favourite addition is crisp-fried Chinese crullers. I first tasted this breakfast in Singapore, once with fish and another time with pork.

WASH AND DRAIN the rice, put it into a saucepan with the water and stock, and bring to the boil. Then reduce the heat, cover the saucepan and simmer for 1 hour or until the rice is very soft.

Meanwhile, remove skin and any bones from the fish fillet, cut into thin slices and mix with the sesame oil, salt and ginger. If using chicken breast, cut into fine shreds and marinate as for the fish.

When porridge is cooked to a thick, creamy consistency, stir in the fish or chicken and cook for 1 minute or just long enough to turn slices white and opaque. Ladle into bowls and let each person choose the accompaniments preferred.

Note: The crisp-fried onions are sometimes available at Asian stores, being the small purple shallots (or 'red onions' as they are called in Asia), finely sliced and fried until golden brown. If preparing them at home, fry in plenty of oil, stirring constantly. Drain, and save the oil to use as a flavouring in many dishes.

Serves 6
1 cup short or
  medium-grain rice
4 cups (1 litre) water
2 cups (16 fl oz) stock
salt and white pepper to
  taste
375 g (12 oz) firm white
  fish fillets or chicken
  breast fillets
2 teaspoons sesame oil
1 teaspoon salt
½ teaspoon finely grated
  ginger
Accompaniments:
finely chopped spring
  onions (scallions)
fresh red chillies, seeded
  and sliced
finely chopped fresh
  coriander leaves
light soy sauce
crisp-fried onions

Cut fish into slices.

Stir fish into creamy rice.

Hainan Chicken Rice

This is a meal in itself, as it comprises rice, soup, chicken and dipping sauces.

WASH THE CHICKEN. Remove fat from the cavity and cut off and discard the tail and wing tips. Wipe with paper towels, and rub salt within the cavity and all over the bird.

In a saucepan just large enough to hold the chicken, bring to the boil at least 8 cups of water. Add the spring onions, celery leaves, peppercorns, sprigs of coriander and 2 teaspoons of salt.

When the water boils, lower the chicken into the pan breast downwards. Let the water return to the boil, then reduce the heat so that it just simmers; cover the pan tightly and simmer for 25 minutes. Remove from heat and leave chicken in the liquid with the pan still tightly covered for a further 45 minutes to finish the cooking.

While chicken is simmering, wash the rice and leave it to drain in a colander for 1 hour.

Lift out and drain the chicken; reserve the stock for cooking the rice and for the soup. Rub the chicken all over with about 2 teaspoons of the measured sesame oil. When cool enough to handle, chop into bite-size pieces and reassemble on serving platter. Cover with foil and keep warm.

Heat the remaining sesame oil and the peanut oil in a heavy saucepan with a well-fitting lid and on medium heat, fry the garlic, ginger and onion, stirring until they are golden (take care they do not burn). Remove 1 tablespoon of this cooked oil and reserve it for one of the dipping sauces.

Add the rice to the pan and fry for a minute or two, stirring until the grains are coated with oil. Add 4 cups of strained chicken stock, and bring to the boil. Add 2 teaspoons of salt and stir well; then turn the heat very low, cover the saucepan tightly and cook for 15 minutes without lifting the lid. Remove from heat and allow to stand, covered, for a further 10 minutes.

Sauces: For one dipping sauce, combine the sliced chilli and the dark soy sauce. For the second dipping sauce, combine crushed chilli, grated ginger, and the reserved tablespoon of cooked oil. These sauces may be served in individual sauce dishes – the two combinations being kept separate.

Soup: Bring the remaining strained stock to the boil. Add the shredded wongah bak or washed and drained bean sprouts, and light soy to taste; and remove from heat after it has boiled for no longer than 30 seconds. Sprinkle coriander on top and serve in a soup tureen.

Each person takes a bowl of rice and eats it with chicken dipped in one of the sauces. Soup is ladled over the rice as desired, or sipped between mouthfuls of chicken and rice.

Serves 5–6
1 × 1.5 kg (3 lb) roasting chicken
salt
2 spring onions
2 sprigs celery leaves
few black peppercorns
few sprigs fresh coriander
500 g (1 lb) long-grain rice
2 tablespoons sesame oil
3 tablespoons peanut oil
4 cloves garlic, sliced
4 slices fresh ginger
1 onion, sliced
stock from cooking the chicken
Sauces:
2 fresh red chillies, sliced
4 tablespoons dark soy sauce
2 tablespoons sambal ulek or freshly ground red chilli
2 tablespoons finely grated fresh ginger
cooked oil from the recipe
Soup:
stock from cooking the chicken
dash of light soy sauce
1 cup shredded wongah bak (or other Chinese cabbage) or bean sprouts
2 tablespoons finely chopped fresh coriander

Rub sesame oil all over the simmered chicken.

Add washed and dried rice to garlic, ginger and onion.

Stir shredded wongah bak into soup stock.

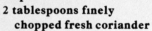

Steamed Rice Cups with Mixed Meats

Serves 8–12

8 dried Chinese mushrooms

1 tablespoon dark soy sauce

2 teaspoons sugar

4 teaspoons sesame oil

2 lap cheong

250 g (8 oz) cooked chicken or barbecued pork

500 g (1 lb) glutinous rice or short-grain rice

2 tablespoons light soy sauce

1 tablespoon peanut oil

½ teaspoon crushed garlic

½ teaspoon finely grated fresh ginger

½ cup Master Sauce (see page 91)

3 teaspoons cornflour (cornstarch)

Steam lap cheong.

Apart from the 'small eats' served in a Chinese breakfast, there are substantial offerings like this. Use rice bowls to mould the rice – or if you wish to make them more dainty, use Chinese tea cups.

SOAK THE MUSHROOMS in hot water for 30 minutes. Then discard the mushroom stems and slice the caps. Put ¾ cup (6 fl oz) of the mushroom soaking liquid into a small saucepan, add the sliced mushrooms, the dark soy sauce, sugar and 2 teaspoons of the sesame oil. Simmer, covered, for 10 minutes.

Place the lap cheong in a colander, and steam for 10 minutes; when cool enough to handle, cut into thin diagonal slices. Dice the chicken or pork.

Place the rice in a saucepan with 4 cups of water. Add the light soy sauce and the remaining 2 teaspoons of sesame oil. Bring to the boil quickly, then turn heat very low, cover the saucepan and cook for 20 minutes.

In a wok, heat the peanut oil and fry the garlic and ginger until golden. Add the Master Sauce and the mushroom liquid, bring to the boil, and thicken with the cornflour mixed with a little cold water. Add the mushrooms, lap cheong and diced chicken or pork. Heat through. Remove from heat and stir into the rice.

Fill small cups, pressing the rice mixture firmly, then unmould and serve. If prepared beforehand, steam the rice mixture in cups until heated through.

Note: If no Master Sauce is on hand, substitute a sauce made from ¼ cup of dark soy, ¼ cup of dry sherry, 1 teaspoon of sugar, and 1 teaspoon of sesame oil.

Cut lap cheong into diagonal slices.

Fill cups with rice mixture and unmould.

Wheat Noodles

Noodles made from wheat flour and eggs are the most popular. Generally sold in 500 g (1 lb) packets, each packet consists of seven or eight bundles. Allow one bundle per person. Unlike rice noodles and bean starch noodles, wheat noodles are always boiled before frying.

Boiled noodles: An important point is that the bundles of noodles must be soaked in hot water for about 10 minutes before dropping them into boiling water. This is not mentioned in the cooking instructions, yet it makes cooking them so much easier. As the bundles soften, the strands separate and the noodles cook evenly, but if they were dropped straight into boiling water the outside would cook while some strands would stick together in tough clumps. If the noodles are loose packed, the soaking is not necessary.

Soak noodles in hot water before boiling.

Bring to the boil a large saucepan of lightly salted water with 1 tablespoon of peanut oil added to prevent boiling over. Drain the soaked noodles in a colander and add to the fast-boiling water. When the water returns to the boil, cook fine noodles for 2 to 3 minutes; wide noodles for 4 to 5 minutes. Test frequently and do not overcook. They should be *al dente*.

Run cold water into the pan, drain immediately in a large colander, and run cold water through the noodles to rinse away excess starch and stop the cooking process. Drain thoroughly.

Soft fried noodles: Sprinkle the well-drained noodles with 1 tablespoon of peanut oil and 2 teaspoons of sesame oil, and toss well. Spread them on a large baking tray and allow to dry in the air for about 1 hour.

Heat a wok or large heavy frying pan, and when very hot, add 3 tablespoons of peanut oil. When the oil is very hot, coil the noodles into the pan to make a round or oval cake. Reduce the heat to medium, and fry, shaking the pan but not stirring, until the base is golden. Turn the noodles over and fry the other side. If it is necessary to add a little more oil, drizzle the oil down the sides of the wok and allow it to become hot before it reaches the noodles. Cook for a further 5 minutes or until golden, then transfer to serving dish.

Soft fried noodles are ideal for serving as a base with any stir-fried and well-sauced foods, either singly or in combination.

Fresh wheat noodles: It is possible to buy fresh wheat noodles in some Asian stores. They need only the briefest cooking in boiling water before they are used in soups or soft fried. If preferred, they may be steamed over boiling water. Allow 10 minutes steaming time.

Some varieties of wheat noodles – for example, the thick yellow Hokkien noodles – are already cooked and need only to have boiling water poured over them in a colander.

Combination Chow Mein

Serves 4

250 g (8 oz) fine wheat
   noodles
1 chicken breast
125 g (4 oz) barbecued
   pork
125 g (4 oz) bean sprouts
125 g (4 oz) snow peas
1 teaspoon crushed garlic
1 teaspoon finely grated
   fresh ginger
1 cup shredded Chinese
   cabbage
6 spring onions (scallions)
   in bite-size lengths
1 can winter bamboo
   shoot, cut into strips
peanut oil
Sauce:
¾ cup (6 fl oz) stock
2 tablespoons light soy
   sauce
2 tablespoons oyster sauce
2 teaspoons sesame oil
3 teaspoons cornflour
   (cornstarch)

This dish of soft fried noodles with mixed meats is very popular. Some westernised versions use crisp fried noodles instead, but this isn't correct. The noodles should be chewy and just slightly crisp on the outside when they have been fried.

COOK THE NOODLES as described on page 130. Drain, toss with oil, and spread on a tray to dry.

Skin and bone the chicken breast, and cut the meat into fine shreds. Cut the barbecued pork into narrow strips. Wash and drain the bean sprouts, discard loose skins and pinch off any straggly tails. String the snow peas. Have all meat and vegetable ingredients ready.

In a bowl, combine the stock, soy sauce, oyster sauce and sesame oil.

Heat a large heavy frying pan and when hot, add 3 tablespoons of peanut oil and fry the noodles on medium heat until crisp and golden on one side (about 5 minutes). Turn them and fry their other side. Remove from heat and keep the noodles warm in the frying pan.

Heat a wok, add 2 tablespoons of peanut oil and swirl to coat the wok. Add garlic and ginger, and stir for a few seconds. Add the chicken, and stir-fry until the chicken changes colour. Add the pork and vegetables, and toss for a further 2 minutes. Add the mixed sauce ingredients, and bring to the boil.

Mix the cornflour smoothly with 2 tablespoons of cold water, add it to the wok and stir until the sauce boils.

Pour over noodles and serve hot.

Spread cooked noodles on a tray to dry.

Cut barbecued pork into narrow strips.

Turn the fried noodles when golden.

Bean Starch Noodles with Pork

Put the noodles in a large bowl, cover with boiling water, then leave for 20 minutes or until soft and transparent. Strain and cut into short lengths with a sharp knife.

Soak the mushrooms in hot water for 30 minutes, squeeze dry, discard stems, dice finely.

Cut the pork into small dice. Mix the wine, soy sauce, salt, stock and cornflour together in a small bowl.

Heat a wok over high heat, add the peanut oil and swirl it around the wok. When the oil is hot, add the pork and mushrooms and stir-fry until cooked and brown. Add the spring onions and ginger, stir for a few seconds; then add the chilli bean sauce and the chopped chilli, and cook over medium heat for a minute or until the mixture looks and smells cooked.

Add the seasonings and sauce mixture, and stir until it comes to the boil. Then add the noodles and simmer, stirring, until all the liquid has cooked down. Stir in the coriander leaves and serve at once.

If desired, garnish with a chilli flower and extra coriander leaves.

Bean Starch Noodles

Transparent bean starch noodles: These fine noodles are also known as cellophane noodles, bean threads, silver threads, spring rain noodles, harusame or fenszu. For a crisp garnish, fry in the same way as rice vermicelli, straight from the packet. For use in soups or braised dishes, soak in hot water or cook in boiling water for 15 minutes or until tender.

Bean starch is also available in large round **sheets**. Soak, cut into strips, and cook in boiling water as directed in recipes.

Serves 4–6

125 g (4 oz) bean starch noodles
6 dried Chinese mushrooms
185 g (6 oz) boneless pork
1 tablespoon Chinese wine or dry sherry
1 tablespoon light soy sauce
1 teaspoon salt
¾ cup light stock
1 teaspoon cornflour (cornstarch)
3 tablespoons peanut oil
4 spring onions (scallions), finely chopped
2 teaspoons finely grated fresh ginger
2 tablespoons chilli bean sauce
1 large fresh red chilli or red capsicum (pepper), seeded and finely chopped
3 tablespoons chopped fresh coriander leaves

Cover bean starch noodles with boiling water.

Cut into short lengths.

Chop the fresh coriander.

Stir-Fried Noodles, Hokkien Style

Hokkien noodles are thick, yellow wheat noodles sold fresh in Asian stores, usually in 500 g (1 lb) bags. This mixture of noodles, vegetables and mixed meat and seafood is a one-dish meal.

POUR BOILING WATER over the noodles to cover them, leave for 1 minute, then drain well in a colander.

Steam the lap cheong over simmering water for 5 minutes or until soft. Allow to cool, then cut into slices. If using pork, cut into small dice.

Shell and de-vein the prawns. Clean and slice the squid. Rinse the bean sprouts and pinch off the straggly tails.

Heat a wok, add 3 tablespoons oil and swirl to coat. Fry the garlic over low heat until golden. Stir-fry the bean sprouts for a few seconds. Add meat and seafood, and stir-fry until they change colour (about 1 minute). Add noodles, and fry until heated through.

Add soy sauce, vinegar, chilli sauce and stock or water mixed together; and cook, tossing, until the liquid has evaporated. Then remove to a dish.

Rinse the wok, heat it again and when hot, add the remaining 1 tablespoon of oil. Pour in the beaten eggs seasoned with salt and pepper; fry quickly, stirring, until firm. Turn off the heat, chop the egg into small pieces with the edge of a wok chan. Return the fried noodle mixture to the wok and toss together. Finally, scatter the garlic chives or spring onions over and serve, garnished with the chillies and celery leaves.

Serves 4
500 g (1 lb) fresh yellow noodles (Hokkien mee)
2 pairs lap cheong or 200 g (7 oz) cooked pork
250 g (8 oz) small prawns, raw or cooked
250 g (8 oz) fresh squid (optional)
250 g (8 oz) fresh bean sprouts
4 tablespoons peanut oil
2 teaspoons finely chopped garlic
2 tablespoons dark soy sauce
2 tablespoons Chinese white vinegar
2 tablespoons sweet chilli sauce
2 tablespoons stock or water
salt and pepper to taste
4 eggs, beaten
2 tablespoons chopped garlic chives (koo chye) or green part of spring onions (scallions)
Garnish:
2 tablespoons chopped tender celery leaves
2 fresh red chillies, seeded and sliced

The Hokkien noodles.

Add meat and seafood to the stir-fried bean sprouts.

Vegetarian Soup Noodles

Soak the dried mushrooms in hot water for 30 minutes. Discard the mushroom stems, and cut the caps into fine strips; reserve 6 cups (1.5 litres) of the soaking water (if necessary, make up the quantity with fresh water). Soak the wood fungus in cold water for 10 minutes; then cut into small pieces, trimming off any gritty portions.

Cut the bean curd into small dice or strips. Combine the light soy sauce, sesame oil and sugar, and toss the bean curd in this mixture.

Wash the carrots and cut wedge-shaped sections out of them, lengthways, then slice across to give flower-shapes. String and slice the beans very thinly. String the snow peas. Cut leaf ribs of the cabbage into bite-size pieces, and finely shred the leaves; keep leaf ribs separate from the shredded leaves. Slice broccoli stems and divide head into flowerets.

Cook the noodles as described on page 130, drain and divide among six soup bowls.

Heat a wok, add the peanut oil and when hot, fry the chopped spring onions and garlic for a few seconds, stirring, but do not let them darken. Add the mushrooms, the sliced leaf ribs of Chinese cabbage and the broccoli stems and fry for 1 minute longer. Add 6 cups of water including the mushroom soaking water, and the seasoning ingredients; bring to the boil and simmer, covered, for 5 minutes. Add the carrots and beans, and cook for a further 3 minutes. Then add the snow peas, wood fungus, shredded cabbage leaves and broccoli flowerets and cook 1 minute longer.

Dissolve the cornflour in 3 tablespoons of cold water, and stir it into the soup until it boils and thickens. Drizzle in the beaten egg and stir gently so that it sets in fine shreds. Add the bean curd and heat through. Ladle the soup mixture over the noodles and serve hot.

Serves 6
8 dried Chinese mushrooms
2 tablespoons dried wood fungus
1 square pressed bean curd
2 tablespoons light soy sauce
2 teaspoons sesame oil
1 teaspoon sugar
2 small carrots
12 green beans
125 g (4 oz) snow peas
8 leaves Chinese cabbage (wongah bak)
250 g (8 oz) broccoli
375 g (12 oz) fine egg noodles
2 tablespoons peanut oil
12 spring onions (scallions), chopped
2 teaspoons finely chopped garlic
3 tablespoons cornflour (cornstarch)
3 eggs, beaten
Seasonings:
2 tablespoons light soy sauce
3 tablespoons Chinese wine or dry sherry
2 teaspoons sesame oil
1 teaspoon salt
1/4 teaspoon ground white pepper

Cut the pressed bean curd into small dice.

Cut carrots into flower shapes.

Divide cooked noodles among soup bowls.

Rice Vermicelli with Prawns

Soak the vermicelli for 10 minutes in hot water; drain in a colander. Wash the mustard cabbage, trim off and discard the leaves, and cut the leaf ribs into thin strips. Shell and de-vein the prawns and, if they are large, cut in two lengthways. Mix together the garlic, ginger, wine, oyster sauce, light soy and stock.

Heat a wok, add the peanut oil and swirl to coat the sides of the wok. Add the prawns, stir-fry until they change colour, then transfer them to a bowl containing the sesame oil. Mix thoroughly.

Re-heat the oil in the wok, add the sliced cabbage and stir-fry for 1 minute. Add the mixed liquids and cook for a further 2 minutes.

Add the vermicelli and toss until heated through. Return the prawns to the wok, toss to mix well, and serve immediately.

Serves 4

250 g (8 oz) rice vermicelli
6 leaves mustard cabbage
  (gai choy)
500 g (1 lb) raw prawns
1 clove garlic, crushed
1 teaspoon finely grated
  fresh ginger
1 tablespoon Chinese wine
  or dry sherry
1 teaspoon oyster sauce
1 tablespoon light soy
  sauce
½ cup stock
salt to taste
3 tablespoons peanut oil
1 teaspoon sesame oil

Soak vermicelli in hot water.

Cut gai choy into strips.

Rice Noodles

Fresh rice noodles: Sa ho fun and chee cheong fun are sheets of fresh rice noodles which are sliced into strips, then heated by pouring boiling water over them. Drain, then stir-fry with other ingredients or simply serve with a sauce.

Dried rice noodles: There are various kinds of dried rice noodles and, depending on the variety, many have to be soaked in cold water for 30 minutes or longer. Drain, drop into fast-boiling water, and boil for 6 to 10 minutes, testing frequently. As soon as they are tender, drain in a colander, and rinse well in cold running water so that they cannot continue to cook in their own heat. Drain once more. Fry or heat in soup before serving.

Dried rice vermicelli: Rice vermicelli has very fine strands and cooks very quickly. Depending on the recipe, they should be cooked in boiling water for 2 minutes or else soaked in hot water. Drain well.

If a crisp garnish is required – for example, a base for presenting prawn fritters or other dishes – use rice vermicelli straight from the packet, frying small amounts at a time in deep hot oil. The oil should be hot enough to make the rice vermicelli puff and whiten as soon as it is immersed. If not hot enough, it will become leathery; but if too hot, it will brown; so it does take a little practice to be able to judge the right heat. Lift out quickly on a wire strainer and drain on absorbent paper.

Fresh Rice Noodles with Sauce

Cut the rice noodles into thin strips. Put them into a bowl and cover with boiling water; cover the bowl and leave for 5 minutes. Drain in a colander.

Place the noodles in a large serving bowl, add all other ingredients and toss lightly until well mixed. Serve on a bed of shredded lettuce and garnish with tomato flowers and coriander.

This snack can be turned into a light meal by adding shreds of cooked pork, chicken, shelled prawns and bean sprouts, or chopped spring onions.

Serves 4

500 g (1 lb) twin rice
   noodles (chee cheong
   fun)
1 tablespoon Chinese
   barbecue sauce
1 tablespoon light soy
   sauce
1 tablespoon dark soy
   sauce
1 tablespoon oyster sauce
2 teaspoons sesame oil
2 teaspoons sweet chilli
   sauce
2 tablespoons toasted
   sesame seeds

Cut rice noodles into slices.

Drain the soaked noodles.

Agar-Agar and Noodle Salad

It is possible to make a meatless version of this salad, substituting strips of bean curd for the chicken, or simply omitting it. An ideal cold dish for picnics or light meals.

SOAK THE AGAR-AGAR for at least 2 hours in cold water. Drain well and cut into finger-length strips. Cook the noodles in plenty of lightly salted boiling water until just tender, testing a piece every now and then to make sure they don't overcook. Run cold water into the pan and drain in a colander.

Combine the beaten eggs with salt and spring onions. Heat a small heavy frying pan. Pour 1 tablespoon of peanut oil into a saucer, dip a piece of kitchen paper in it and lightly grease the base of the frying pan. Pour in just enough of the egg mixture to make a thin omelette; cook on low heat just until set, without browning, then turn it out on to a plate. Continue until all the egg is used. Allow to cool.

Heat a wok, add the remaining tablespoon of peanut oil and fry the garlic for a few seconds, not long enough to brown it. Add the bean sprouts and toss for 30 seconds, then remove from heat. Allow to cool.

In a large serving bowl, toss together the agar-agar, noodles, bean sprouts and chicken.

Combine the sesame oil and soy sauce to make a dressing, pour it over the ingredients in the bowl, and toss to distribute the dressing.

Roll up the omelettes (like a Swiss roll), cut them into narrow slices, and add to the bowl. Cover and refrigerate. Just before serving, garnish with the coriander and spring onions and strips of ham.

Serves 6
15 g (½ oz) refined agar-agar strips
250 g (8 oz) egg noodles
2 eggs, beaten
½ teaspoon salt
2 spring onions (scallions)
2 tablespoons peanut oil
½ teaspoon crushed garlic
250 g (8 oz) fresh bean sprouts
strips of cold, cooked chicken
2 tablespoons sesame oil
3 tablespoons light soy sauce
3 tablespoons chopped fresh coriander leaves
3 tablespoons sliced spring onions (scallions)
matchstick strips of ham (optional)

Drain the agar-agar and cut into pieces.

Toss agar-agar, noodles, bean sprouts and chicken.

Roll up omelettes and cut into slices.

Sweets and Breads

Chinese meals don't feature desserts, but there is no denying it is a pleasant custom and most Chinese restaurants humour their patrons by providing something to end the meal on a sweet note such as Toffee Apples, Almond Bean Curd or that incredibly un-Chinese concoction, Fried Ice Cream.

Most often though, sweets are eaten as between-meal snacks.Chinese sweetmeats are turned out in factories and are quite cheap and easy to purchase. Don't expect the labels to enlighten you about the contents. 'Peanut Cake' for instance, is flat, crisp and rather similar to Middle Eastern halva. I have eaten it, freshly made, in Eastern cities but it loses nothing when packaged in transparent paper and sealed in packets.

Then there are brittle, toffee-like bars of sesame seeds and sugar; deep fried cookies made of thin, crisp batter; flaky pastry or soft, freshly steamed yeast buns with fillings of sweet bean paste or lotus nut paste. Moon cakes, which sell by the thousand during the period leading up to the Moon Festival, are made from pastry pressed into a patterned wooden mould, filled with a solid core of chopped preserved fruits and nuts then richly glazed and baked. Those most prized have, in the centre, the yolk of a salted duck egg. Not to everyone's taste, perhaps.

There is also a variety of dried fruit, prettily wrapped in paper and labelled either 'Preserved Plum', 'Preserved Prune', or 'Honeyed Apricot'. They are sweet but also salty, a combination that is strange at first, then addictive. Dried lychees in their shells are totally different from the fresh or canned fruit. The shell becomes thin, brittle and easily cracked while the fruit has turned dark, rather like a large, round raisin.

Walnut and date 'cake' is a sticky, fudge-like creation but pleasant and not too sweet. A word of advice: some of these sweets are wrapped twice and the inner wrapping which looks like fine food wrap is really rice paper which is meant to be eaten with the sweet. Don't try to remove it – it defies all efforts.

Perhaps the most popular ending to a meal is fortune cookies. These too are sold in packets, but are so much nicer if freshly made so a simple recipe is included in this chapter. Here, too, are recipes for the buns, steamed breads and mandarin pancakes which are meant to be served with savoury dishes.

Left: clockwise from front left: Fortune Cookies (see page 140), dried lychees, small peanut candies, dates, Steamed Flower Rolls (see page 143), almond flavoured cakes, dried plums (paper wrapped), moon cakes, deep fried pastries, dried plums, date toffee, sesame brittle, peanut cakes.

Fortune Cookies

Makes 12–14
2 egg whites
4 tablespoons caster
   (powdered) sugar
2 tablespoons cornflour
   (cornstarch)
2 tablespoons flour
½ teaspoon vanilla
   essence
1 teaspoon peanut oil

Have the 'fortunes' typed on short strips of paper, ready to enclose.

Preheat the oven to 180°C (350°F/Gas 4). Prepare baking trays by brushing with oil and dusting with cornflour; tap off excess cornflour. Mark two circles about 9 cm (3½ inches) across, using a bowl or mug.

Lightly beat the egg whites just until frothy. Add the sugar and mix it in. Stir in sifted cornflour and flour. Add the vanilla essence and the peanut oil, and stir to combine. Place 2 teaspoons of the mixture on each circle and spread evenly with a knife.

Bake in the preheated oven for about 8 minutes or until evenly golden in colour. Immediately remove the cookies, one at a time. Place a 'fortune' on the cookie, press the edges together and bend the folded side of the cookie over the edge of a bowl to give it a twist. Immediately fold other biscuit. If it has firmed, return it to the oven to soften. If the biscuits are too hot for you to handle, use a cloth or oven mits. Allow to cool on wire racks, and store in an airtight container.

Spread cookie mixture on prepared trays.

Place 'fortune' in cookie and press edge together.

Bend cookie over edge of bowl.

Mandarin Pancakes

Serves 4–5
2 cups (8 oz) flour
¾ cup (6 fl oz) boiling
    water
1 tablespoon sesame oil

These delicate pancakes are traditionally served with Peking Duck, but are also used to enclose a variety of fillings such as shredded pork or chicken. The filling is seasoned with a dab of rich-flavoured sauce, then rolled up and eaten.

MEASURE THE UNSIFTED FLOUR into a bowl. Bring water to the boil and pour at once on to the flour, stirring with chopsticks or the handle of a wooden spoon for a few minutes. As soon as it is cool enough to handle, knead for 10 minutes until the mixture is a soft, smooth dough. Put the dough on a board and cover with a bowl, then let it stand for at least 30 minutes.

Roll the dough into a cylindrical shape and cut it into ten slices of equal size. Keep covered with plastic wrap to prevent drying out.

Take one dough slice at a time and cut into two equal pieces. Form each to a smooth ball, then roll out on a lightly floured board to a circle about 8 cm (3 inches) in diameter. Brush one circle lightly with sesame oil, taking it right to the edge of the circle. Put the second circle on top of the first one and roll again, both circles together this time, until the pancakes are 15–18 cm (6–7 inches) across. They must be very thin. Cover each pancake with plastic as it is made.

When they are all rolled out, heat a heavy frying pan or griddle and cook the pancakes one at a time on the ungreased surface. Cook over low heat until the pancake develops small bubbles. Turn it frequently so that it cooks on both sides. A few golden spots will appear.

Remove from pan and gently pull the two circles apart. The sesame oil they were brushed with makes this quite easy. Pile the cooked pancakes on a plate, and cover tightly or they will dry out. Pancakes should be soft and pliable, not brittle.

To reheat, arrange the pancakes in a steamer lined with a clean tea towel, cover and put over simmering water for 1–2 minutes. To serve, fold each pancake into quarters.

Serve with Crisp-Fried Boneless Duck (see page 101), Mu Shu Pork (page 113) and similar dishes.

Stir boiling water into flour using chopsticks.

Knead dough until soft and smooth.

Oil one circle of dough and cover with another.

The cooked pancakes separate easily.

Steamed Silver Thread Rolls

Makes 8 rolls
15 g (½ oz) fresh yeast
3 tablespoons sugar
2½ cups (10 oz) flour
½ teaspoon baking powder
sesame oil

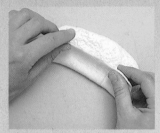

Brush rectangle of dough with sesame oil and fold in half lengthways.

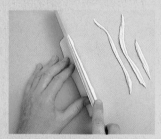

Brush with more oil, fold again and cut into strips.

Place on an oblong-shaped piece of dough.

Bring edges together and pinch to join.

Crumble the yeast into a bowl, gradually stir in the sugar and then add 1 cup (8 fl oz) lukewarm water, stirring until sugar and yeast are dissolved.

Sift the flour and baking powder and add to liquid, mixing to a fairly firm dough. Knead on a floured surface for 5 minutes or until dough becomes smooth and elastic.

Rub a large bowl with a little oil and place the dough in the bowl, turning once so that the top of dough is lightly oiled. Cover with plastic wrap and leave in a warm place to rise until double in bulk (about 2 hours).

Turn the dough out on to a floured surface and knead for 5 minutes. Then divide it into 16 equal portions.

Roll one portion to an oblong shape 15 cm × 10 cm (6 inches × 4 inches). Brush lightly with sesame oil and fold in half lengthways, then brush with more oil and fold again. Cut into fine strips. Roll another portion of dough to a thick oblong shape, wide enough to wrap around the strips and about the same length. Place the strips on the oblong dough, bring its edges together and pinch to join them. Place seam side downwards.

Prepare seven more dough rolls in the same way. Leave to rise in a warm place for 30 minutes. Steam in a bamboo steamer for 15 minutes.

Serve with rich dishes such as Crisp-Fried Boneless Duck (see page 101) and Mu Shu Pork (page 113).

Steamed Flower Rolls

Prepare the dough as for Silver Thread Rolls, leave it to rise for about 2 hours, knead a second time, then divide into halves. Set one portion aside.

On a lightly floured board, use a floured rolling pin to roll out one portion of dough to a rectangle 40 cm × 30 cm (16 inches × 12 inches). Brush the entire surface with sesame oil, then starting at the long side, roll up the dough to form a cylinder. Cut into 2.5 cm (1 inch) slices. There should be 16 of these.

Place one roll on top of another and with a chopstick press firmly in the centre. The rolled edges will open like the petals of a flower. Repeat, to make seven more dough flowers. Place in a lightly oiled steaming basket, and steam over boiling water for 8 to 10 minutes. Repeat with remaining portion of dough.

Rolls may be made beforehand and reheated by gently steaming for 2 to 3 minutes.

Note: If a bamboo steamer is not available, use a large saucepan and place the rolls on a plate above the water level, but line the lid with a tea towel to prevent condensation dropping on to the rolls and spoiling their appearance. Also, when steaming is finished, turn off the heat but leave for a minute or two before lifting the lid to prevent a rush of cold air causing the steamed dough to shrink or wrinkle.

Makes 16 rolls
15 g (½ oz) fresh yeast
3 tablespoons sugar
2½ cups (10 oz) flour
½ teaspoon baking powder
sesame oil

Brush rectangle of dough with sesame oil and roll up.

Cut into slices.

Place one roll on top of another and press a chopstick firmly in the centre.

Steam in a lightly oiled basket for 8 to 10 minutes.

Wonton Wrappers

These are readily available in Chinese specialty shops, but if you can't get to one, or if you would like to try your hand at making them, here's how.

SIFT THE FLOUR and salt into a large bowl. Make a well in the centre.

Beat the egg lightly with ½ cup (4 fl oz) water, and pour it into the well in the flour. Mixing from the centre, with a fork, gradually work in the flour. Knead into a ball, then turn it out on to a well-floured surface and knead the dough for 5 to 6 minutes until smooth. Cover with a damp cloth and leave to rest for 30 minutes.

Cut the dough into four portions, and roll each portion out on a well-floured surface. Using a ruler, cut dough into 8 cm (3 inch) squares. Stack in piles, dusting liberally with cornflour to prevent sticking. Wrap the piles in plastic and store in the refrigerator.

Cut dough into quarters and roll out.

Cut the thinly rolled-out dough into squares.

Makes 40–50 wrappers
2 cups (8 oz) flour
½ teaspoon salt
1 egg
extra flour
cornflour (cornstarch)

Deep Fried Date Wonton

These crisp sweetmeats will keep for a week in an airtight container.

CHOP THE DATES finely. Chop the nuts too. Combine dates, nuts, grated rind and just enough juice to make the mixture hold together. Form into small cylinders which will fit on the pastry squares diagonally, leaving enough pastry to twist at each end like a cracker.

Place the date rolls on the pastry, take one corner and tuck it under, then roll up to enclose the filling. Twist the ends, putting a finger in the pastry to give it a Christmas cracker shape.

When all the wonton are wrapped, heat 3–4 cups (24–32 fl oz) peanut oil in a wok and fry a few at a time, turning them, until they are golden brown all over. Lift out with a wire spoon and drain on paper towels placed on a wire rack. When cool, sprinkle lightly with icing sugar. Store in an airtight container.

Note: If preferred, use canned lotus nut paste or sweet bean paste for the filling.

Makes about 50
250 g (8 oz) pitted dates
60 g (2 oz) walnuts or
   almonds
1 teaspoon finely grated
   orange rind
1 tablespoon orange juice
250 g (8 oz) wonton pastry
   squares
peanut oil for deep frying
icing (confectioners')
   sugar for dusting

Twist ends of filled pastries.

Sesame Balls

Makes 20
125 g (4 oz) pitted dates
2 tablespoons sesame
   paste
375 g (12 oz) sweet
   potatoes
1¼ cups (5 oz) flour
4 tablespoons brown sugar
1 egg white
1 cup (5 oz) sesame seeds
peanut oil for deep frying

Put the dates into a small saucepan with water to cover. Bring to the boil and boil for 1 minute. Drain, then mash the dates to a paste. Blend in the sesame paste.

Peel the sweet potatoes, cut them into chunks. Put them into a saucepan with water to cover, bring to the boil and simmer for 20 to 30 minutes until the potato is tender. Drain well, then mash and force through a sieve. Measure 1¼ cups.

Sift 1 cup of the flour into a bowl, add the 1¼ cups of sweet potato and mix with a fork. The mixture will be lumpy at this stage.

Heat the sugar with 1 tablespoon of water until boiling, stirring to dissolve the sugar. Add this hot syrup to the flour and potato mixture. Form it into a dough, adding a little more flour if necessary. Knead lightly on a floured surface for 1 minute.

Divide the dough evenly into 20 portions and roll each portion into a ball. Flatten the ball with the palm of your hand. Place a teaspoon of the date-sesame mixture in the centre. Shape into a ball, completely enclosing the paste. Repeat with the remaining dough and filling.

Place the balls in an oiled steaming basket and steam over gently boiling water for 10 minutes.

Dip the balls in lightly beaten egg white and then roll them in sesame seeds.

Heat a wok, add oil for deep frying. When hot, fry the sesame balls until golden. Drain and serve warm or cold.

Put spoonful of date filling on flattened dough.

Steam the balls in an oiled basket.

Dip the balls in egg white and roll in sesame seeds.

Toffee Yams with Black Sesame Seeds

This is a popular dessert and impressive. It may also be done with apple or with firm ripe bananas, peeled and cut into chunks but not pre-cooked.

PEEL THE SWEET POTATOES and cut them into diagonal slices. Drop them into a large saucepan of boiling water for 5 minutes. Drain and cool.

Beat the egg in a medium-sized bowl, add ⅔ cup of cold water, and beat again until combined. Then tip in all the flour at once and beat vigorously until the batter is smooth. Allow the batter to stand while preparing the glaze.

Glaze: Heat the oil in a saucepan, add the sugar and ½ cup (4 fl oz) cold water. Place the saucepan over medium heat. Do not stir at all. If you do, the sugar will crystallize and the glaze will not be clear. Let the sugar mixture bubble until it starts to turn golden around the edge of the pan. Then stir in the sesame seeds and turn the heat as low as it will go. Or remove the saucepan from heat, replacing it from time to time if sugar begins to harden before the sweet potatoes have been dipped.

As the sugar cooks, start to heat the oil for deep frying. Try to have the oil hot and the sugar glaze ready (that is, deep golden) at the same time. If the oil is put over a moderate heat, this should not be difficult.

When a haze begins to rise from the surface of the oil, drop pieces of sweet potato into the batter, turn to coat them completely, then take one piece at a time with chopsticks, a fondue fork or fingers and drop it into the oil. Deep fry until the batter is golden, then lift out with a slotted spoon and put it straight into the saucepan containing the glaze. Do two or three pieces at a time, turn them so that the glaze coats their entire surface, then lift out on to an oiled plate.

Take immediately to the table, together with a bowl containing cold water and ice cubes. Each person takes a piece of glazed yam and drops it into the bowl. The glaze will harden and become brittle almost at once. Lift out quickly and eat. If left to stand too long, the glaze will melt and the batter will become leathery.

Deep fry the battered yams until golden.

Glaze 2 to 3 pieces of yam at a time and lift onto an oiled plate.

Guests dip glazed yams into cold water before eating.

Serves 6
500 g (1 lb) sweet potatoes
1 egg
1 cup (4 oz) flour
peanut oil for deep frying
Glaze:
1 teaspoon peanut oil
1½ cups (12 oz) sugar
1 tablespoon black sesame seeds

Almond Bean Curd

Serves 4–6
4 teaspoons powdered agar-agar, or 1 cup soaked and drained agar-agar strands
1 can sweetened condensed milk
1–2 teaspoons almond essence

Put 4 cups (32 fl oz) water into a saucepan, sprinkle the agar-agar over and bring to the boil. Boil and stir until the agar-agar is dissolved. Powdered agar takes only a couple of minutes to dissolve, but the strands take longer.

Add the condensed milk and almond essence, and stir well. Pour the mixture into a large shallow glass dish or a large cake tin. Allow it to cool and set, then chill.

Cut it into cubes or diamond shapes, and serve by itself or with canned fruits or freshly made melon balls.

The agar-agar powder and dried strands of agar-agar.

Cut the chilled mixture into shapes.

Glossary

AGAR-AGAR: A setting agent made from seaweed. Available in powder form in packets from Asian grocery stores. Also available in strands. Use either type for jellies, but for dishes like Agar-Agar and Noodle Salad, only the strands are suitable. See photograph on page 147.

BAMBOO SHOOT: Sold in cans either water-packed or braised. Unless otherwise stated, the recipes in this book call for the water-packed variety. After opening can, store in a bowl of fresh water in the refrigerator, replacing water daily, for up to 10 days.

BARBECUED PORK: This may be bought freshly cooked in most Asian stores. Usually made from fillets or neck of pork marinated in a spicy, salty and sweet mixture and cooked in special ovens. See photograph on page 131. May be made at home (see page 110).

BEAN CURD: (dow foo) Fresh soft bean curd, made from soy beans, is available in the refrigerator section of Asian stores, ready to use. Immersed in cold water which should be changed daily, it will keep for 2 to 3 days in the refrigerator. It has a soft, custard-like texture. See photograph on page 74. No substitute.

Dried bean curd: (tiem jook, fu jook pei) Comes in thin, flat sheets or rounded sticks. Needs no refrigeration, keeps indefinitely in wrapping or jar, needs to be soaked before use.

Fried bean curd: (dow foo pok) Sold in the refrigerator section in Asian stores, usually in plastic bags. See photograph on page 50. Can be kept under refrigeration for 3 or 4 days.

Hard bean curd: (pressed bean curd) Also sold fresh, is firmer and has a different flavour. See photograph on page 50. Good protein in vegetarian meals. Store in refrigerator for 2 or 3 days. Canned variety may be used in braised dishes, but the fresh is infinitely better.

Red bean curd: (nam yu) Also known as bean curd cheese because it is fermented and very strong flavoured. Used in small amounts to add flavour to special dishes. See photograph on page 100. Keeps indefinitely in jar.

BEAN SAUCES: There are many kinds of bean sauce, salty, sweet and hot. The most basic are mor sze jeung (ground bean sauce), smooth and thick, and min sze jeung, a thick paste of mashed and whole fermented soy beans. The most popular sweet bean sauce is hoi sin jeung. The hot bean sauces (mostly used in Szechwan style dishes) are chilli bean sauce, hot bean sauce and soy chilli sauce. Some are oily, some are not. All these bean sauces are too thick to pour. Use the one specified in the recipe for the best results.

BEAN PASTE (SAUCE), SWEET: Sweet and salty thick sauce or paste which is sold in jars and keeps indefinitely. See photograph on page 19. Depending on which brand you buy, it could be described as 'paste' or 'sauce' or 'sweet ground bean sauce'. Play it safe and also look for the Chinese name which is tin min jeung to distinguish this sauce from dow saah the sweet bean paste (also called 'sweetened black bean paste' or 'sweet mashed bean paste') which is used as a filling for steamed buns.

BEAN SPROUTS: Green mung beans are used for bean sprouts. They are sold fresh in most Chinese stores and in certain supermarkets and health food stores. The canned variety are not recommended. Substitute thinly sliced celery for crunchy texture, though flavour is different. Fresh bean sprouts may be stored in refrigerator for a week in plastic bag, or cover with water and change water daily.

BEAN STARCH NOODLES: Also known as bean threads or cellophane noodles. Fine transparent noodles made from the starch of green mung beans. See photograph on page 35. They may be soaked in hot water or boiled, or for a crisp garnish are deep fried straight from the packet. Cut with scissors—they're tough.

BEAN STARCH SHEETS: Made from green mung beans, these round sheets are soaked in hot water, then cooked until soft. See photographs on page 28. Sold in Chinese stores in plastic bags, in dried form the starch sheets keep indefinitely.

BLACK BEANS, SALTED: Soy beans, heavily salted and preserved in cans. See photograph on page 79. Rinse before using to prevent oversalting. After opening, store in refrigerator, for as long as six months. Pour a little peanut oil on top if it seems to dry out.

CHILLI OIL: Sold in small bottles, it is oil impregnated with the pungent flavour of chillies and is used in small amounts. Keeps for about a month after opening. If unobtainable, make some by heating about a cup of oil in a wok and adding some dried red chillies. If using the large chillies, use 12 and if using the small chillies, which are much hotter, use less. Fry the chillies for a minute or so, until they turn dark, remove wok from heat and leave until quite cold before straining the oil and storing in a bottle.

CHILLI SAUCE: Chinese chilli sauce is different from other chilli sauce. Substitute Tabasco or other hot pepper sauce, not one of the sweet chilli sauces. Keeps indefinitely.

CHILLI SAUCE, SWEET: Milder but still fairly pungent, the sweetened chilli sauce usually has added garlic and ginger. Substitute either unsweetened chilli sauce mixed with a little sugar, crushed garlic and ginger, or tomato sauce with a generous dash of Tabasco.

CHINESE CABBAGE: There are a number of Chinese vegetables which are all called 'cabbage' but are quite different in appearance and flavour. Each has been photographed in the recipe to make identification easy, but here are descriptions which may help when purchasing.

Bok choy: Chinese chard, with silvery white leaf ribs and very dark green leaves, it is one of the milder flavoured vegetables. See photograph on page 52.

Gai choy: Mustard cabbage, so called because of its strong, mustardy tang. Recognise it by its brilliant green colour and the way its leaves curve from the central stalk. See photograph on page 30.

Gai larn: Chinese broccoli or kale. Dark green stems and leaves, with white flowers. Select young plants with buds rather than flowers. Thicker stems may need peeling and splitting. See photograph on page 36.

Wongah bak: The most popular, widely known Chinese cabbage is variously called Tientsin cabbage, celery cabbage and Peking cabbage. It is most delicate in flavour and has broad white leaf ribs with pale green leaves packed together tightly. It may be eaten raw, but most often is lightly cooked with other ingredients. See photograph on page 37.

Choy sum: Flowering cabbage, rather like gai larn in appearance but its flowers are yellow and the stems do not have a thick tough skin. See photograph on page 104.

Like all members of the cabbage family, Chinese cabbages are most plentiful in the cooler months. Soak in cold water and wash very well, especially where the leaves join the stem, to ensure all sand and any insecticides are rinsed away. All Chinese vegetables should be cooked briefly so their colour intensifies and the texture remains crisp.

CHINESE VINEGAR: (ba tso) There is more than one kind of Chinese vinegar, some light in colour, others quite dark, sweet and spicy. Used in cooking or as a dip. Substitute: these vinegars are milder than western wine or cider vinegars, so quantities must be adjusted or vinegar diluted if a substitution is made.

CHINESE WINE: (Shao hsing) Rice wine which may be substituted with dry sherry.

CORIANDER, FRESH: (Chinese parsley) This is the green herb as distinct from the dried seeds used as a spice in curry mixtures. Dark green, with leaves resembling flat Italian parsley, this pungent herb is used widely in Chinese cooking. See photograph on page 132. Store in tightly closed plastic bags in crisper section of refrigerator. Really fresh bunches which have not been wet (or if they have, are thoroughly dried on absorbent paper) will keep for about two weeks. No substitute for flavour, but use parsley for a garnish.

CUCUMBER SLICES IN SYRUP, PRESERVED: Rather like shoelace shreds of melon and carrot in a heavy syrup, they are also sometimes labelled 'sweet pickled cucumber' or 'preserved melon shreds'. See photograph on page 68. They will keep indefinitely in a covered jar.

CUMQUATS IN SYRUP: Most commonly sold in 390g jars, these tangy citrus fruits go well with salty sauces. See photograph on page 115. If you have a cumquat tree, you could try using the fresh fruit, first removing the seeds. Keeps well in its own jar and needs no refrigeration. Substitute glacé orange slices.

DRIED SHRIMP: Used as a seasoning rather than a main ingredient, because drying gives them a concentrated flavour. Soak as directed. Sold by weight in packets, they keep almost indefinitely in sealed packets or in a tightly covered jar after opening. No substitute.

FISH MAW, DRIED: (fish tripe, yu toe) The dried stomach lining of large fish, it is purely a texture ingredient, has no fishy taste or smell and looks, in its dried state, like a puffy, cream-coloured sponge. See photograph on page 45. Soak as directed in individual recipes. No substitute.

FIVE SPICE POWDER: A combination of ground anise, fennel, cinnamon, cloves and Szechwan pepper, it gives distinctive flavour in cooking and is also used as a dip, combined with salt. Inexpensive, keeps well in tightly covered jar.

GARLIC CHIVES: (koo chye or gau choi) these long, flat green leaves have a strong flavour, half-way between garlic and spring onions. Store in paper in the crisper section of the refrigerator. Some Chinese stores sell these together with other fresh vegetables.

GINGER ROOT: A basic seasoning in Chinese food. Buy fresh root ginger from Chinese food shops, greengrocers, supermarkets. Store by freezing in a plastic bag, peeling and bottling in a jar of dry sherry (store in refrigerator); or burying in moist soil and watering frequently. Dig up a piece as needed, replace remaining ginger root in soil and keep moist. If you are able to buy it frequently, store in the crisper section of the refrigerator where it will keep fresh for about three weeks. Ginger is also available sliced in cans and this is the best substitute for fresh ginger. Do not use powdered ginger as a substitute.

GINGER, RED: Ginger slices in heavy syrup, coloured a bright red. Add to Chinese dishes as a flavouring and garnish. No substitute.

GLUTEN: Gluten is the protein part of wheat, and a very fine flour made from it is available in health food stores. Prepare as described on page 53. Used in vegetarian dishes, it is a meat substitute and absorbs other flavours though it has very little flavour of its own. Fried bean curd is a reasonable substitute.

HOI SIN SAUCE: A thick, sweet, spicy, reddish brown sauce made from beans, garlic, spices. Keeps well in a covered jar.

LAP CHEONG: Dried Chinese-style sausages filled only with spiced and slightly sweetened lean and fat pork. See photograph on page 129. Will keep without refrigeration. Steam for 10 minutes until soft and plump, cut into thin slices to serve or to include in dishes. Quite expensive compared to ordinary western style sausages because they contain no fillers. Substitute barbecued pork.

LILY BUDS, DRIED: (Also known as golden needles, dried tiger lillies) these dried buds are long and narrow with a delicate flavour. They are said to be nutritious. See photograph on page 113. Sold in cellophane packets, they need at least 30 minutes soaking in hot water. Will keep well if stored in an airtight jar. Substitute another bland vegetable, or omit from recipe.

LONG BEANS: Pictured on page 63, these are sometimes known as snake beans or yard beans. Dark green, thin beans are preferable to thicker, paler green ones as they are sweeter and more tender. Substitute very tender young French beans.

LOTUS ROOT: Sometimes available fresh. Peel, cut into slices and use as directed. See photograph on page 114. Dried lotus root keeps well, must be soaked in hot water for at least 20 minutes, with lemon juice added to preserve whiteness. Canned lotus root is readily available, but for the recipes in this book you don't buy the canned lotus root in sugar syrup.

MELON, BITTER: (Fu gwa) This gourd looks like a green cucumber but with a pebbly-textured, very glossy skin. See photograph on page 108. When ripe it is a pretty golden colour with bright red seeds, but the time to eat it is when it is green in colour and only half mature. The flavour is bitter, but pleasantly so, combining well with strong-flavoured sauces and meat or seafood. No substitute.

MELON, FUZZY: Pale green, rounded ends with a narrower centre, the fuzzy melon is about a handspan in length and, true to its name, has a covering of prickly white fuzz. See photograph on page 44. Scrub well and peel thinly so the flesh is still tinged with green. It may be used interchangeably with winter melon as the texture and delicate flavour is very similar. Substitute peeled, seeded cucumbers.

MELON, WINTER: A dark green, watermelon-like gourd which can grow up to 50kg in weight! No wonder it is usually sold by the slice. The neutral flesh takes flavours from other ingredients. Substitute fuzzy melon or cucumber.

MSG (MONOSODIUM GLUTAMATE): While it is not used in this book, I include it in the glossary because it has long been regarded as essential to Chinese cooking. This is not so. It is only when ingredients are of poor quality or soups and sauces have been watered down that it is resorted to, and there are none of those practices here. Besides, the chemical compound which looks like white crystals of coarse salt, not only acts as a catalyst on the taste buds but has unpleasant effects on some people. I never use it.

MUSHROOMS, DRIED CHINESE: There are two types of dried Chinese mushrooms, one which is called Flower Mushroom because of the petal-like indentations on its upper surface. The caps of these mushrooms are thicker and meatier than the other type which are sometimes known as 'love letters' or winter mushrooms. The flavour is similar, but flower mushrooms are more expensive. However, they are the best kind to use because of their chewy texture. Dried mushrooms keep indefinitely in a closed packet or jar, are sold by weight (sometimes in packets or boxes) and though the price seems frighteningly high, a little goes a long way and even the tough stems and soaking water (they need at least 30 minutes soaking in very hot water) can be used to flavour stocks. See photograph on page 23. No substitute. Do not substitute dried European mushrooms, the flavour is different.

OLIVE NUTS: Delicate, sweet-flavoured nut with crumbly texture. See photograph on page 93. Be careful not to cook these on too high heat as they burn easily. Expensive. Store in freezer. Substitute cashew nuts or pine nuts.

OYSTER SAUCE: Adds delicate flavour to all kinds of dishes. Made from oysters cooked in soy sauce and brine, this thick brown sauce keeps indefinitely. Once opened, store in refrigerator.

PEPPERY TURNIPS, (chilli radish): A strong-flavoured condiment which is used in some dishes to give a fiery tang. See photograph on page 89. Keeps well in covered jar. Substitute small amount of chilli bean sauce.

PICKLES, CHINESE MIXED: Small onions, gherkins, cucumber, ginger and other selected vegetables in a vinegar, sugar and salt pickling mixture. See photograph on page 96. Substitute pickled gherkins and onions if necessary.

PLUM SAUCE: Sweet and spicy and sometimes slightly hot, this sauce is based on plums, chillies, vinegar, spices and sugar. Use as a dip. Keeps indefinitely in a covered jar.

ROCK SUGAR: Pale amber lumps of raw sugar which are used to give a subtle sweetness and glaze to some dishes. See photograph on page 13. Since it comes in quite large pieces, wrap one in a cloth and crush with a meat mallet before measuring. Substitute granulated sugar or raw sugar crystals.

SAMBAL ULEK: This paste of hot fresh red chillies is the easy way to adding the pungency of ground chillies without the work and the burning fingers. Sometimes labelled in the old Dutch Indonesian way, 'sambal oelek'. Same thing. Keeps well. After opening, store in refrigerator.

SESAME OIL: This oil is extracted from toasted sesame seeds, giving it a rich amber colour and totally different flavour from the lighter sesame oil sometimes sold in health stores. For the recipes in this book, purchase sesame oil from Chinese stores. Use in small quantities for flavouring, not as a cooking medium.

SHARK FIN: Unless you want to precede the eating with three days' work, use the canned shark fin! See photograph on page 40. The dried fins are very expensive, must be soaked and cooked for hours. Even the canned fins (which are split into shreds of gelatinous cartilage) are not exactly cheap. Substitute boiled bean starch noodles if you must, but shark fin is a prestige ingredient for banqueting and no substitute is really acceptable.

SNOW PEAS: Also known as sugar peas. Sold fresh in season, these are mainly a speciality of Chinese market gardeners but large seed companies now sell the seeds in packets under the name of sugar peas. They are never cooked for longer than a minute or two and are eaten pod and all. The French name for them is mangetout. They are sometimes available frozen, but lack the delightful crispness of the fresh peas. Store fresh snow peas for a few days in a plastic bag or in a bowl of water in the refrigerator.

SOY SAUCE: Indispensable in Chinese cooking, this versatile sauce enhances the flavour of every basic ingredient in a dish. Different grades are available. Dark soy sauce is used in most instances, but light soy is used when cooking chicken or seafood, or in soups where the delicate flavour and colour of the dish must be preserved. Keeps indefinitely. Usually sold in large or small bottles, but if purchased in a can, decant into a bottle.

SPRING ONION: (scallions) The member of the onion family known as a shallot in Australia is correctly called a spring onion almost everywhere else. Use the straight, slender onions without large, well developed bulbs.

SPRING ROLL WRAPPERS: Thin, white sheets of pastry sold in plastic packets. Usually frozen. Unused wrappers may be refrozen. Large wonton wrappers may not be substituted.

STAR ANISE: One of the prettiest seed pods, it looks like a reddish brown, eight-petalled flower. See photograph on page 121. Used in stocks or master sauces for red-cooked dishes, it imparts a licorice flavour. Keeps indefinitely in covered jar. Inexpensive. No substitute.

STRAW MUSHROOMS: Unlike dried mushrooms with their strong flavour, these mushrooms are as delicately flavoured as champignons. They are shrouded in their own little 'tent' which envelops the stalk and cap with a thin skin. Sold in cans. See photograph on page 94.

SZECHWAN PEPPERCORNS: Also known as anise pepper, Chinese pepper, faah jiu. A small reddish-brown dried berry, smaller than black peppercorns and not as hot. They give a tingling, numbing sensation when placed on the tongue. See photograph on page 92. Dry roast in a dry pan until fragrant, about 5 minutes over low heat, stirring now and then. Pound in mortar and pestle or with cleaver. Keeps well in an airtight bottle.

TANGERINE PEEL, DRIED: (gom pei) Gives citrus fragrance to dishes. Expensive, so when mandarins or tangerines are in season, save the peel, scrape away any white pith and dry the peel in the sun or in a very low oven. Store airtight. Fresh peel may be used as a substitute.

TWIN RICE NOODLES: Chee cheong fun. These already cooked rice noodles look for all the world like two rolled-up white linen handkerchiefs wrapped in plastic. See photograph on page 123. They need only to be sliced through and heated either by pouring boiling water over or by steaming in a colander before combining with other ingredients. Look for them in the refrigerator section of Asian food stores. If not in stock, substitute sa ho fun (rice noodles in flat sheets, folded) which are also treated the same way before incorporating in a recipe. They are sometimes used as a wrapping for a savoury filling. Keep refrigerated for a few days.

WALNUTS: Peeled walnuts are sold by weight in Chinese grocery stores and are perfect for using in fried dishes, as the thin skin which turns bitter through cooking has been removed. If peeled walnuts are not available, use the canned, salted walnuts also sold in Chinese stores. These do not need further cooking.

WATER CHESTNUTS: Sometimes available fresh, the brownish-black skin must be peeled away with a sharp knife, leaving the crisp, slightly sweet kernel. Available in cans, already peeled. After opening, store in water in refrigerator for a week changing water daily. No substitute. See photograph on page 118.

WONTON WRAPPERS: Small squares of fresh noodle dough bought from Chinese stores. Refrigerate, well wrapped in plastic, for a week. See photograph on page 230.

WOOD FUNGUS: (Cloud ears, tree ears, wun yee, jelly mushrooms.) Sold by weight, wood fungus in its dry state looks like greyish black pieces of paper. Soaked in water for 10 minutes, it swells to translucent brown shapes which explains why it is called 'cloud ear'. See photograph on page 35. No flavour, but its resilience is greatly prized as a texture ingredient and it takes on flavours from other foods. Cook only a minute or two. Keeps indefinitely in dried form, and for a few days in the refrigerator after soaking. No substitute.

Index